THE CREATIVITY INFUSION

THE CREATIVITY INFUSION
How Managers Can Start and Sustain Creativity and Innovation

R. DONALD GAMACHE

and

ROBERT LAWRENCE KUHN

1817

Harper & Row, Publishers, New York

BALLINGER DIVISION

Grand Rapids, Philadelphia, St. Louis, San Francisco
London, Singapore, Sydney, Tokyo, Toronto

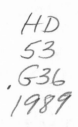

International Standard Book Number: 0-88730-343-9

Library of Congress Catalog Card Number: 89-27595

Printed in the United States of America

Library of Congress Cataloging in Publication Data

Gamache, R. Donald, 1935-
   The creativity infusion : how managers can start and sustain creativity and infusion / R. Donald Gamache and Robert Lawrence Kuhn.
      p. cm.
   ISBN 0-88730-343-9
   1. Creative ability in business. I. Kuhn, Robert Lawrence.
II. Title.
HD53.G36   1989
658.4'09—dc20   89-27595
                                                                                    CIP

To all my girls—Kathleen, Nanette, Lisette . . . and Mariette
—R. Donald Gamache

To all my family—Aaron, Adam, Daniella . . . and Dora
—Robert Lawrence Kuhn

CONTENTS

viii   CONTENTS

PREFACE

This book is about a lifetime's experience. Clearly, then, the contributors include all those people who contributed to that experience—good and painful. (Many times the most valuable of our lessons were the hardest to learn.) My greatest thanks go to my greatest "enablers"—my wife and daughters, who were there at the end of every day (when I wasn't away earning and learning). They weren't always a fan club, though sometimes when I "needed," they were. But they always helped me keep perspective—especially in the headiest moments.

Special thanks go to all my co-workers through the years, the many people with whom I collaborated on the hundreds of client assignments. I tried to teach them everything I knew; they taught me everything they were learning.

Thanks go to Irving G. Calish, my friend, partner, and INNO-TECH's cofounder. We shared an important part of our lives—personal and professional—until his death in January 1985. Ken Van Dyck and the founders of the Foresight Group—Sven Atterhed, Lennart Boksjö, and Gustaf Delin—played key roles in my business development. Finally, to those who specifically contributed their experiences, ideas, and insights to this book, I owe thanks. They include my friends at INNOTECH. Kurt W. Eastman, INNOTECH's Services Division president, was of great help with Chapters 7 and 8. Matthew B. Calish contributed to Chapter 9. John L. Ehrler, my lifelong friend and an INNO-TECH director, shared his experience in Chapter 6. William S. Parker had many years of hard-earned experience to pass on in Chapter 5. Finally, Dr. Oswald V. Simpson, Joel K. Pondelik, and Pete R. Klinkowski all made important contributions to Chapters 1, 2, and 4, respectively.

As in many noteworthy undertakings, the real force is behind the scenes. For the equivalent of working full-time, three-plus months, my secretary and assistant, Lila M. Forte, deciphered every written and spoken word. In addition, she often served as cheerleader, prod, and co-conspirator. And with every draft of every chapter she affixed a different "happy face." (They served as amulets to drive away the pedantic, I hope.) And when Lila couldn't do what needed to be done on time, she got her friends Lisa Timman and Sharon Roman to help.

To my executive friends who contributed their lifetimes of experiences and learning to each chapter in the sections titled "Another View from the Real World," their contributions require more than mere thanks. They made not only this book but my business lifetime happen—always with grace and humor but, most importantly, with friendships.

R. Donald Gamache

INTRODUCTION

Creativity in business is both thinking and doing. Without the former, it is unfocused and inefficient; without the latter, abstract and irrelevant. This book is about making profitable innovation for the real world focused, efficient, concrete, and relevant.

Creativity in business is surprise, breakthrough, leaps of logic, and sudden jumps. It propels companies and catapults careers. It is the way of dynamic change, potent growth, and competitive advantage. This is the frontier, the cutting edge of contemporary commerce. It is intense, gutsy, spirited, and strange. It is also fun—even heroic. Creativity at work, in short, builds strong and successful companies. It wins.

Is being a creative manager the same as being a manager of creativity? No, and the distinction is important. The crux of the difference lies in where the creative action occurs, and this is the heart of the managerial process. A creative manager is himself or herself creative, *producing creative content personally* in the conduct of managerial tasks. A manager of creativity, on the other hand, is *a facilitator of the creative process*, working to generate creative content in others. The skill sets for each are not the same—indeed, there is little overlap—although either one can also be the other.

Furthermore, those who generate ideas are often not the best ones to implement them. Again, skill sets are different. Organizations grow only when personnel increase opportunities for current products and services or produce new ones. All managers should therefore aspire to be creative; and if they cannot personally parent innovation, they should assist subordinates in its gestation. Managers must be sensitive to change and ready to accept new ideas, irrespective of direction or source. This means, by necessity, that existing strategies, structures, systems, and services are not permanent. To think that everything in the organization is replaceable can be unnerving and risky, but those who must maintain the status quo run the higher risk of being overthrown by committed individuals who are not bound by conventional wisdom.*

Robert Lawrence Kuhn

*For further, in-depth discussions of numerous aspects of the creative process in business and organizations, I would recommend, if I may be permitted a personal plug, the *Handbook for Creative and Innovative Managers* (McGraw-Hill, 1988).

THE CREATIVITY INFUSION

1

WHY CREATIVITY DOESN'T START
Barriers of Inertia and Attitude

We start in reverse—backwards in one sense, at the core in another—by first considering why creativity *doesn't* start. The world of innovation and creativity is a positive and optimistic one. It has to be in order to work. Yet it's essential that we know our enemies—barriers to creativity—in order to recognize, manage, and ultimately overcome them. Some are well disguised and diabolically clever. So our task is to alert those managers who are committed to change and growth to the problems that have hurt, plagued, and even killed other organizations.

We don't want to give the impression that these problems are universal. Clearly, many companies are dealing beautifully with the needs and challenges of business growth and innovation. We believe that in many cases they have already identified these enemies and are vigilantly monitoring and working hard to overcome them. We gained our "wisdom" slowly and painfully at the world-famous "Lumps-on-the-Head Institute." It's a hard way to learn, but sometimes—when the book has not yet been written—it's the only way.

Here are our basic definitions:

- **Creativity?** Our core premise is that creativity is the insightful rearrangement of known information.

- **Innovation:** In our lexicon, while creativity deals with getting the idea, innovation relates to commercializing it into new products and services that generate revenues and profits.

SOME CREATIVITY STOPPERS

In the play-cum-movie *Fiddler on the Roof*, there's a show-stopping song titled "Tradition." It extols the virtues of having a long list of stabilizing cultural traditions. True, many benefits to a family or a culture come from Fourth of July picnics and Thanksgiving dinners, but "we've always done it this way" is a major reason why creativity in business doesn't start.

We remember a meeting with the top management group of a European company that had a letter of appreciation from George Washington thanking them for the timely delivery of cannons for use in the American Revolution. We were there to discuss new business opportunities. In their ornate, formal boardroom stood a long, narrow table guaranteed to ruin good group dynamics. No one seated at it could maintain eye contact or feel a sense of involvement with more than two or three people.

Furthermore, on the walls of the room hung portraits of every head of the company going back at least to the fellow who had gotten the letter from George. The room reeked with tradition. But it also dampened any attempt to be creative or discuss ideas or areas that would require change. The figure in each portrait seemed to admonish the current managing director not to make a mistake and risk destroying all the hundreds of years of stability and tradition the company had enjoyed.

During one of the meetings with these folks we first encountered the one-two punch for not doing something new. The set-up punch was, "But we've always done it this way," and the knockout was, "But we've never done it that way." The management group presented both lines as reasons not to change. Suffice it to say, their attempt at identifying new growth opportunities fell flat.

False Security of Success

At least the company just described knew it should be *trying* to do new things. Other companies are less fortunate because they are the victims of success—a success that, unfortunately, had a large component of good fortune in it rather than talent or skill. One such example emerged during a growth program conducted for a West Coast manufacturer of a component critical to the logging industry. The company enjoyed a monopoly position and, consequently, obscene profitability. Even the company's executives admitted that their business "beat stealing." However, they had enjoyed little growth and wanted to explore new avenues. Nevertheless, when any "normal" business idea or area was addressed—one requiring change, risk, investment, and less-than-obscene profits—it quickly paled by comparison with their usual practices and was summarily rejected.

Here was a clear case of what we've come to call an "intellectual exercise": the spirit is willing, but the flesh is weak. So after several mutually frustrating rounds, the project was abandoned. Interestingly, a number of years later, a foreign competitor appeared on the scene to attack the company's monopoly. Now the executives could no longer enjoy the luxury of the past because they were severely threatened. This created enough pressure to force the organization to again attempt to move into new areas.

However, the culture continued to play a dominant and constricting role. Rather than taking a meaningful step into a new opportunity, the executives approved new products that were comfortable, nonthreatening, tiny excursions—products that in reality would never have a significant impact on their future growth or survival.

So if your organization is successful, ask yourself why. Be honest: If good fortune is a major contributor, luck is a poor excuse for complacency. In our more than twenty years of working with companies in the arena of business growth, we have seen many such companies humbled by significant changes in the dynamics of their marketplace. Their past successes, and poorly founded arrogance, would not allow them to acknowledge the threat or act in time.

Today's increasing pace of change does not allow companies the luxury of refusing to acknowledge and react to a potential threat as soon as it surfaces. Delays are either severely debilitating or, as in many cases, fatal.

Fear of Failure

Another reason why creativity doesn't start is the pervasive and potent fear of failure that exists in almost all organizations. It's difficult to believe that many executives don't realize that to do something new you have to *do something new.* Unfortunately, doing something new always entails risks. These risks range from the frightening "bet your company" variety to the often petty, political career concerns of people pushed to change. But a fear of change and risk taking can cripple an individual or an organization.

Because of the potential negative career impact, the fear of making mistakes is often legitimate. Many companies have, by some mechanism, ensured that the downside of failure far exceeds the upside potential of success. Therefore, a fairly reasonable and rational attitude would be: Why try something new and take the risk?—especially when mistakes are more "visible" than inaction.

In many companies a rich lore seems to prove that you get coveted promotions by maintaining a low profile and staying the course for many years; otherwise, you will haunt the corporate halls along with others who have tried, failed, and suffered career death. So many executives believe that inaction is safer than action, mistakes kill careers, and low-profile, riskless performance garners rewards. Clearly, these beliefs help explain why creativity doesn't start.

Comfort in the Known

A successful solution tends to be repeated. Furthermore, it continues to be repeated for a while even after it no longer works. If you tried something yesterday and it worked, you avoid risk by doing it the same way today. We saw this principle in action at a division of a major West Coast aircraft manufacturer.

When we were called in during the mid-1970s, management was feeling the pinch of reduced government spending. This clearly seemed the time to pursue nongovernment business creatively and aggressively. So a program was launched that led to some exciting opportunities. After feeble and snail-paced attempts to move these forward, however, the new vistas were ultimately abandoned. Why? In the interim, government contracts had turned upward again, and rather than risk the unknown, the managers delightedly scurried back to the security of their known products and relationships.

We've seen this scenario unfold many times over the years. Because of a downturn in its core market, a company faces trouble. The managers recognize their overdependence on traditional products and markets and rationally begin to identify other opportunities. This process continues until the market turns up again. The managers then abandon all efforts at diversification—and sigh with relief.

ORGANIZATIONS MUST CHANGE OR DIE

A company that loses its ability to change in order to meet the needs of today's ever-changing marketplace is doomed. Only about one-third of the companies on the original Fortune 500 list are there today. So neither size nor success guarantee survival.

All sectors of the business world must pursue rational, strategic change. It's an irrefutable fact that if any organization stops changing, it's only a matter of time before its relevance to the world ceases to exist. This is easy to see in markets with high-tech products, but less visible in slower-moving areas. In fact, it may seem that some industries—for example, natural materials—can largely ignore change.

An interesting example that proves the contrary comes from northern Sweden. An iron mining company, known internationally as LKAB, was situated on some of the world's richest iron deposits. Its ore was so sought after that potential customers would wine and dine management! "Sales" meant allocating their production among favorite customers, and the concept of marketing didn't exist. Given the circumstances, this was easy to understand. But times change—even if you're "only" digging material out of the ground.

Technology proved disruptive. Developments in steel making produced processes that were intolerant of the mineral phosphorus. And the rich Kiruna ore, unfortunately, had unacceptable levels of this element in major areas of the ore body. Suddenly, a group of executives who felt they were immune to change became the victims of it. But technology became the hero. Developments triggered by NASA's exploration of space allowed the production of reliable on-board testing systems that enabled the operator of a huge underground loader to discriminate between high- and low-phosophorous ore.

THE NEED FOR NEW INFORMATION

If one thinks about it, companies are designed for today's businesses. This is quite apparent when we examine their complement of employees. For example, a consumer product company typically needs manufacturing technology to produce its products, and marketing and sales skills to turn them into cash. Their staffing, then, qualifies them to do what they're already doing very well. It also enables them to vary slightly at either end of the marketing or manufacturing spectrum. That's why

so many companies' new products are actually just minor variations on their old ones. But when it comes to doing something
significantly new—something that departs from an organization's core capabilities—companies are far less successful. Aside
from the pervasive human and cultural problems, there is the
genuine problem of *the need for new information.*

People in an organization represent its human data base. If
new ideas result from the insightful rearrangement of known
information, and the company's "data base" changes little over
a period of time, all possible permutations of this information
will eventually be explored and either rejected or acted upon.
That explains why during the course of a year, a certain number
of executives say to a creativity consultant or to themselves,
"We just completed our annual idea hunt, and we got the same
old ideas. How come?"

The problem occurs because they are continually reprocessing
and rearranging essentially the same information. Therefore, for
an organization to do something really new, it needs new information to manipulate promising new combinations—blendings
of existing capabilities and new information. Not realizing this,
some executives feel that because they have thousands of employees, they can produce all the new products and future
growth opportunities they'll need.

But logic and evidence to the contrary exist. Even if a company has tens of thousands of employees, after a while each
individual's information becomes homogenized as he or she is
assimilated into the culture. Soon the employees begin talking
company jargon—shorthand, often replete with alphabet-soup
code letters.

Unfortunately, rather than aggressively going outside to
seek new inputs, many organizations develop an "NIH"—not-
invented-here—culture. Some companies practically forbid contact with the outside world by their research or commercial
development people. The attitude is, We're paying you guys to
come up with the new ideas, so why should we spend additional
monies outside?

THE LOSS OF PERSPECTIVE

In addition to the need to add new information to an organization are the problems of overfamiliarity and lack of perspective. These insidious developments blind an organization to its own potential strengths and capabilities, which, if focused upon, could lead to new opportunities.

A psychological principle is that the familiar tends to become invisible. A simple exercise you could do right now to prove this is—DON'T LOOK AT YOUR WATCH! Now, attempt to draw it from memory as accurately, and in as much detail, as possible. Of the thousands of executives we've had try this, almost all made significant errors of omission or commission—even to the point of drawing a round watch when they actually had a square one, or vice versa.

Scandinavians use the term *home blind* to describe this rather normal phenomenon. The principle behind it is that our senses tend to react to change rather than to the steady state.* So familiarity tends to make something "invisible." Little is more familiar than one's own face, and many men shave theirs every day. How many strokes do you think it takes most men to shave in the morning? Think about it for a minute, and come up with a number before reading further. Most men answer in the twenties or thirties.

In reality, it takes well over a hundred strokes. So another reason creativity doesn't start is that we tend not to appreciate the potential value of our existing capabilities and strengths because they've become commonplace. When we take them for granted, they become invisible.

A law of Newtonian physics tells us that a body tends to remain in its current state—in motion or at rest—until acted on by an outside force. A growing company requires additional

---

*Psychological reactions to change are derived from the physiology of the sensory system, where changing stimuli cause the greatest excitement and constant stimuli trigger "habituation" when the same stimuli are repeated, with progressively weakening impact.

people. These people bring precisely the fresh, new perspectives and additional information that fuel continuing growth. A stagnant company becomes even more stagnant, particularly as its better or best people leave.

TAKING A SHORT-TERM VERSUS A LONG-TERM VIEW

Another factor that has a major impact on creativity—and often a swift and devastating one—is the shift to a short-term focus at the expense of the longer-range outlook. The most uncreative organizations have a very near term vision that totally dominates everyone's activities. Such a view holds that the future of the company lies in the next six months or year.

This ambience immediately squelches the development of anything that will not pay immediate dividends. And the plans that are drawn up and implemented leave no room for deviation; they must be followed exactly. Short-term demands create a very tight structure, leaving little leeway for originality or experimentation. There's no time to waste on fooling around with something that won't pay off tomorrow. Although dedicated and creative individuals will always find a way, such a culture makes it extremely difficult for innovation to happen.

After a long career in new business development, Dr. Oswald Simpson, an INNOTECH vice-president, believes strongly that "creative and innovative individuals exist in almost any organization . . . but recognizing the severe constraints placed upon their ideas and visions, they are far more likely to leave to find a more fertile arena than to spend their time, effort and energies battling a system that is working against them."

So when a company's management turns, for whatever the reason, from long- or even medium-term planning to an overemphasis on short-term goals, the demise of creativity will soon follow. In the many growth programs that have been run for them, European companies have consistently established two themes in their criteria that are not typical for U.S. companies:

(1) a concern for the continued employment of their work force and (2) a patient, longer-term orientation.

Bias Towards Short-Term Incentives

The way most managements tend to get compensated for performance also contributes to a short-term mentality, with its deleterious effects on creativity and innovation. (Remember, in our lexicon, *creativity* describes the idea-getting process, whereas *innovation* relates to the commercializing process.)

Almost every management incentive system extant in the United States emphasizes short-term performance, usually at the expense of the longer-term payback that comes from investing in new products and new opportunities. In fact, short- and long-term goals often clash directly. We've heard executives say more than once that they would be foolish to sacrifice their incentives by investing in an unproven enterprise with an improbable outcome that clearly had far more downside than upside for them personally.

Unfortunately, it is not only the top management of a company that establishes and supports these incentives. The blame extends to the board of directors. In fact, the short-term, profit-oriented focus of some boards is the bane of a management that sees the need for longer-term investments and is willing to undertake the quest.

UNREALISTIC EXPECTATIONS OF R&D

The abbreviation *R&D* is a good example of the problem of "we've always done it this way." Companies have stuck tenaciously to the words *research and development* despite the fact that the great majority of these organizations don't do *any* research—and in many cases don't even do development.

In our increasingly short-term-focused business world, the majority of R&D divisions or departments usually emphasize either technical support of existing businesses or customer service—nothing really new. Yet managers state proudly that they have an R&D organization and, often in the same breath, opine that they're dissatisfied with its "lack of creativity and productivity" in the new product or business development arena.

In reality, the great majority of R&D organizations would be better served by "reframing" them in terms of what they are actually doing, rather than what management thinks or hopes they are doing. "Technical Support," "Customer Service," or some other appropriate label would change the expectations for a hard-working group of people and allow them to receive recognition and rewards for their actual efforts, not criticism under the misnomer of "R&D."

This mislabeling has another negative effect: it results in compartmentalization, the setting up of barriers that have a decidedly negative impact on creativity and innovation. If R&D is assumed to have the responsibility for generating new ideas, it becomes "not my job" in other areas of the organization. Sitting behind this protective shield of not having the personal responsibility for new developments, these people often readily criticize R&D for not producing the new products.

Such criticism also thrives in the marketing-dominated culture typically found in a consumer packaged goods firm. Here, marketing bears the brunt of the responsibility for new product creativity, and all fingers are pointed at it because R&D is merely a vehicle for the technical development of ideas generated by marketing.

It has been proven that cooperation and the free flow of ideas among the various functional areas in an organization greatly enhance creativity. And if we go back to our core premise that creativity is the insightful rearrangement of known information, it logically follows that a broader organizational perspective on new products and business development will bring more and different information to the task.

But many companies have the NIH attitude within their own functional areas. In that case, marketing is far less than receptive to an idea proposed by a "technician," and the development folks hold the NIH view about the meddling of marketing, sales, and even management itself.

POOR "SALESPEOPLE" FOR PROMISING IDEAS

Although a few salespeople are born with the "gift," the great majority receive training or develop their skills over a long period of trial-and-error apprenticeship. Not everyone is an effective salesperson; this seems particularly true of those trained in the sciences. So in defense of some of the naysayers and rejecters, most new ideas are presented in such an amateurish way that only an idiot or a genius would be willing to invest his or her time, money, or career in them.

There are no quick fixes to this problem. But one solution is to have salespeople establish a simple framework or outline for the presentation of an idea. This will help to assure coverage of most, if not all, key factors potentially involved. Also, being aware of the problem can make a manager more patient and receptive when he or she hears a poorly presented idea or opportunity. Instead of summarily rejecting such an idea, the manager might do well to coach the presenter and give him or her another opportunity.

This remedial approach has been successful when working with entrepreneurs or their internal counterparts in seeking funding. They are coached and developed, using practice presentations to a potential financial backer or mock board. These provide the presenter with a valuable learning experience. Coaching and trial-run sessions ultimately produce a more effective presenter and presentation, which both help assure that an idea is accepted, sponsored, and funded (or rejected) based on its merits—and not dismissed because of poor sales techniques or an amateurish presentation.

A willingness to try such approaches is important. If management seems quick and superficial in rejecting a series of ideas from an individual or throughout an organization, the presentation of all ideas, including potentially winning ones, will cease because the culture is viewed as hostile to new ideas and suggestions.

THE DO-IT (ALL)-YOURSELF REFLEX

Another problem that falls into the category of "we've always done it this way" is the deeply ingrained reflex of a company to undertake the development of a promising idea internally, using its own staff. Obviously, if the idea is far enough away from the existing capabilities of the organization, it needs new people to develop that idea efficiently—if at all.

Some companies have an almost pathological concern for secrecy. They feel that if the new plan or product is developed by internal employees, its secrecy is assured. Yet we read of many cases where an employee who helped develop a unique product leaves the organization and takes his or her knowledge to a start-up or competitor. And the record of the courts in ruling for the company over the individual has been abysmal. So secrecy as the reason for internal development has dubious merit.

Given the potential benefits of going outside, companies should at least reexamine their reflex to develop everything internally. We have seen management hire new people, establish a facility, and purchase expensive equipment with long lead times to develop an unproven idea. Clearly, the consequences of failure are enormous in lost time, money, and human trauma when such an effort is finally aborted.

Also, staying the course beyond a rational best effort is more likely to occur because of the massive negative consequences of admitting failure. We have seen numerous projects continued for many years because management did not have the stomach for terminating them.

One such case involved a biotech company that had eight significant research projects under way, all well funded and staffed with bright, dedicated people. The company had yet to achieve any commercial sales, and its "burn rate" was in the many millions of dollars annually. So management could see the company running out of funds. Because no criteria existed to determine the success, failure, or appropriateness of any of the projects, the first step was to develop a tight set of criteria that could be accepted and supported by the top business and technical management.

When the eight projects were examined against the criteria, the company executives found that for the first time they could prioritize them against the best chance of a payback within the desired time frame. Shockingly, three of these well-funded and -staffed projects lacked *any* support from the entire management group and, seemingly, had not had any support for years. But, lacking objective criteria, the managers had no mechanism for killing them without being accused of having purely political motives.

So companies remain oriented to the thinking that goes, "Please, Mother, I'll do it myself!" And "renting" is not often a part of an organization's culture. Yet, in many cases, by "going outside" a company could develop a concept in a fraction of the time for a fraction of the cost, and with more financial control and a far easier decision-making process to terminate a project that became less promising than originally conceived.

We know one highly successful, midsized high-tech company that, since its founding, has contracted several additional generations of its products—along with new related products—by dealing exclusively with exceptionally qualified outside development organizations. Not surprisingly, the president swears by this approach and proudly presents his pioneering way of thinking to other, more traditional executives.

POOR CREATIVITY LEADERSHIP

As in every field of endeavor—military, government, or business—the leader sets the tone for others in the organization. Therefore, creativity often doesn't start because of the leader of the unit and what he or she communicates, consciously or unconsciously, about creativity and innovation. From our experience, we believe that no other single factor is more important in the demise or flourishing of creative productivity.

They Can't Even Spell Kreativity

In sessions with executives we have found that all too many lack any understanding of the fundamentals of creativity. This ignorance is excusable given that certainly less than 5 percent of executives have had any, even quasi-formal, training in creativity. So we say they have a "license to be stupid" about it, just as anyone walking into their companies could be expected to have a license to be stupid about all the arcane knowledge required to run their business successfully. But the fact remains that business executives know almost nothing about creativity. Clearly, this puts them in an extremely difficult situation when they are attempting to *manage* it.

Many years ago we ran a seminar on creative new product development for the American Management Association. It was well attended by high-level executives. At the conclusion of the two-day event an individual who was executive vice-president of a major specialty packaging firm approached us and confessed that before he had left to attend the event, he had written a memo regarding new products and had it disseminated to his people. Now a few days later, having just learned some of the fundamentals of creativity, he stated with chagrin, "Everything I wrote in that memo was wrong." Like this executive, many managers have no concept of how to direct or manage a creative effort yet feel responsible for doing so.

Other leaders recognize that a high degree of potential creativity exists in their organization, and they earnestly hope to do something about it. We believe that almost all organizations lacking in creativity are the victims of the leader's lack of knowledge about how to promote it rather than his or her conscious effort to stifle it.

Resistance to Creativity

Unfortunately, leaders often do oppose fresh thinking and acting. Executives are trained, bred, and encouraged to make good decisions. And good decisions are based on solid information. So executives tend to want to make good decisions based on good information, and if that information can be taken to the third decimal point, that's even better.

Such precision is the antithesis of what creativity, innovation, new products, and new business opportunities are all about. New ideas start as very sketchy, fuzzy, loose, and amorphous— full of unknowns. Expecting the typical executive to entertain all this ambiguity is asking a lot. Consequently, managers make knee-jerk judgments on nearly everything rather than tolerate new, untested ideas.

By analogy, a new idea is like a baby because it clearly cannot feed or defend itself. To achieve maturity, it needs someone's commitment of love, patience, and time. We know that babies cannot be judged against adults. Yet we forget that new ideas cannot be judged against the standards of an existing operating business. If the culture of an organization is going to provide a fertile nursery for the growth of promising "idea babies," the leader must clearly communicate his or her ability both to tolerate some rational degree of ambiguity and to appreciate the creativity that produces it.

Appreciating creativity goes beyond just grudgingly tolerating it. The organization must make room for the creative individual, who is quite often the questioning individual. The individual who asks dumb, probing, unpopular, and sometimes painful questions is far from easy to tolerate or "manage." But if a company's culture is committed to the future, the managers must find the mechanisms for supporting creative people, without their being overly disruptive to the organization and others in it.

LACK OF VISCERAL COMMITMENT

Commitment in any field means staying the course through the bad times. In *The Power of Myth* Joseph Campbell points out that the difference between true love and an affair is commitment. The same is equally true in a company pursuing its own future. If mechanisms are in place with the objective of creating new products or business opportunities, turning them off whenever a downturn occurs is virtually (but not virtuously) "having an affair" with the future. That is, really believing in the future means staying the course through the downturns.

Some companies clearly have never wavered in such a commitment, among them 3M, IBM, and AT&T. Others seem to be in and out of the new product business every few years, proving themselves the unfaithful lovers of the business world. We have seen many times the difference between the *intellectual* commitment to newness and the painful changes it often requires, and a truly gut-level emotional commitment.

Change is never easy, and doing something new always requires change. Getting through the tough parts requires commitment and often courage. We have an inside joke at INNO-TECH that goes, "We'll do *anything* new as long as it's *exactly* like what we're doing."

Several years ago we ran a new product program for a manufacturer of engine valves. For those of you who don't know what an engine valve is, it's a pencil-like rod with a disk stuck to one end that opens and closes an orifice to control the flow of gases in an engine. At the time, the dramatic switch to small cars with small engines had reduced the number of valves required. So management was looking for new business opportunities, and we worked with this group looking for new products. At one point, we learned that their manufacturing equipment was totally *dedicated* to making valves and had zero flexibility for making anything else. Yet they insisted that the new product be made on their existing equipment, and even worse, they weren't ready to modify it or add anything new. Hence, we came to the realization that any "new" product would have to look *exactly* like a valve. By mutual agreement, the new product program was soon aborted. So the commitment of this management group to doing something new was clearly intellectual rather than emotional.

CULTURES CAN BE HOSTILE TO CREATIVITY

An organization must be able to leave a little room for individuals to be different. Taking a behaviorist approach to determining who is truly creative—not just who seems to be—we must look ultimately for results, that is, a creative individual *is* as a creative individual *does.*

This characterization helps managers understand that mavericks are not necessarily creative individuals, nor vice versa. But given the probability that a higher percentage of unconventional (maverick) thinking will come from being truly creative, the truly creative individual is more difficult to fit into the organization. Typically, even if creative people are recognized, they are required to march to the beat of the *same* drummer as everyone else in a company. No creativity from management goes into managing or accommodating them. They're managed in the same way as people who have no difficulty at all living within boundaries.

If a culture is hostile to truly creative individuals, they try to pursue their ideas on their own time. It's not too difficult to see that after a while this can lead to domestic problems. Ultimately, the creative individual pays the penalty for failure personally. Somehow, that doesn't seem fair. So it is the responsibility of management—and again primarily the leader—to be consciously aware of structuring an environment that can encourage creative productivity.

One thing to strive for in a climate conducive to creativity is a certain degree of informality. Formality tends to be a defense of the insecure. An open environment that tolerates the difficult questions or the unconventional, and that fosters camaraderie, leads to mutual support, cooperation, and tolerance. It also tends to allow humor to thrive.

Humor is not peripheral to creative environments. Rather than being a luxury, humor is an essential component of a creative atmosphere. It allows people to say "stupid" things . . . that turn out not to be so stupid. It allows the tentative presenter of an off-the-wall idea to disguise it as a joke.

Perhaps the best way to frame what the right culture should be is to describe what it should not be: The most negative, most hostile, most confining ambience is one where all focus is on the very short term. Consequently, the organization becomes uptight and its components become defensively provincial. Finally, the leader must strive to recognize some best efforts—best *rational* efforts—and not just recognize success. This creates an ambience where freedom to fail is a recognized right. But this freedom to fail must be limited to small failures—not the "bet your company" variety. Some degree of freedom to fail will allow people to be innovative and creatively productive.

ANOTHER VIEW FROM THE REAL WORLD

Mark Spivack

Throughout his twenty-plus-year association with Union Carbide, Dr. Mark Spivack has carried the thread of new product and business development over many assignments. Currently general manager for business development in the Specialty Chemicals Division, he has been a prime mover in the group's diversification efforts, one key piece of which is an internal venturing program. For this program, and with the division's senior management, he worked with the Planned Growth *process to generate success criteria and from this identified a number of promising opportunity areas for the "intrapreneur" to pursue with specific ideas for business opportunities. Also, in the course of his work he has been involved with identifying cultural and organizational issues that are both barriers to and supports for the process of creativity and innovation, and with implementing and managing the changes requisite to growth.*

The Need for Leadership

In observing why creativity and innovation don't start, it is abundantly apparent how much of an influence the top executive can exert. If he wants to make something happen, the odds are high that it will happen. Or if that something doesn't happen, he probably is not at fault. If he only pays lip service to meaningful actions, then all he's going to get is lip service. And for all the money and effort spent, he'll end up with cocktail conversation, nothing more. The troops have an uncanny ability to distinguish whether it's talk or whether it's real—that ability must be a "sixth sense."

The leader—the prime mover for doing new things—does not necessarily have to be the chief executive officer (CEO), although the company's commitment is certainly stronger if he or she is. The leader can be the head of a subgroup in the organization, a major operating or functional group, a division, or whatever. He or she is the "numero uno" of that entity or business unit. But if the direct leadership does go all the way up to the top, the chances for success increase exponentially.

The necessity of active top-level control depends on both how far away from the current business the venturing will be and the size of the expectation. The bigger it is, or the further away it is, the more Number One—the true number one—has to buy into it and lead it. If it's small enough in the overall context of the organization that it can fit neatly within a given operating component where it can't do too much damage or change the strategic direction of the enterprise, then it can be the top dog in that particular component.

So I'm saying that Number One had better be very visible, and he must truly want to make it happen. It's a leadership question. But we must recognize that almost all Number Ones have constraints, even if he or she is the CEO. If it's a private company and the CEO owns all the marbles, then there's little problem. In reality, in most of America and elsewhere, there are other owners—the stockholders. And then there's something called Wall Street. And Wall Street is traditionally short-term and very bottom-line oriented. So when you get into creativity and innovation, things that are for the most part longer-term situations, the time frame is usually a lot longer than Wall Streeters are willing to tolerate—unless they feel it's something that has enormous potential.

Take a look at the investment glamour represented by biotechnology in the 1970s and early 1980s. Then the realization started to hit that biotechnology was not an end unto itself but simply a means of making products. So success in biotechnology was redefined to mean products, not just R&D contracts and hype. And the gleam started to fade.

Interestingly enough, Wall Streeters seem to be more tolerant of things they don't understand well. But in most cases, Wall Street demands a very short term orientation. So one reason creativity has difficulty in starting, and translating to success, is this pressure. Even with the strongest, most creative, aggressive leaders, any reins will constrain actions. And it really takes an unusual person to buck that. Fortunately, they do exist.

Another stumbling block is that the reward systems in most companies reinforce a short-term philosophy. Stock options not withstanding, rewards are generally based on what you did for me within the last year—Did you increase profits? Did you meet budget?—and what you *promise* to do for me in the foreseeable future.

Unlike the independent startup, most systems in larger corporations reward promises. A reward for the proven success of a new product introduced several years ago shows up rarely. So a disincentive for creativity, particularly outside the R&D function, is the reward system. New products are not easy because they take a long-term commitment, and that requires incentives. But there are ways of doing it, such as with phantom stock and profit sharing at the profit center level.

The Need for Patience

A related dilemma is simply patience. Most people will shake their head up and down when the subject of doing new things comes up and say "Yes, risk is high. Yes, it takes a long time. You've got to kiss a lot of frogs to find the prince." Seldom will you find anybody disagreeing. But in short order the actions commonly implemented include a limited number of projects, a slap on the wrist for failure, and the complaint, "Where are the new products?"

What is the average time span from inception to commercialization? It varies from industry to industry. Typically, in consumer product areas the life cycle is short, so the development cycle also has to be short. In the chemical industry, five to seven years are about average. In the aerospace industry, fifteen to twenty years are not unusual. The consequence in the consumer products industry—perhaps with the exception of electronics—is that there are few truly new products. Most are repackagings, reformulations, repositionings, new sizes. But you can put the word *new* on them. Some of these, though, are well done and reflect first-class creativity. Again, success goes back to measurement, rewards, expectations, and the like. So the few things that make it through the daunting process are usually the exceptions. And there is always a champion involved, hiding costs or diverting energy to make something happen, because creativity and innovation sure don't happen by themselves.

One well-worn route used to make something happen is overpromising to get funded, which also addresses the issue of impact. In most larger corporations you'll again have the heads nodding up and down: "Yes, big things start small." And in the same breath is voiced the home-run philosophy—that is, "We can't really afford to fool around with something that is only a few million dollars."

In reality it's a genuine conundrum. To have any impact in even a modest time frame, a Fortune 100 company would need a major hit. Ten million gets lost in rounding a decimal. So that's a damper on creativity too. It is difficult, if not awesome, for someone who wants to start something new to imagine even in his wildest vision how it's ever going to make any impact. And it is disheartening.

Rigid Cultures

Several of the factors already discussed relate to culture. There are many others. Organizations, just like individuals, have grown up in certain ways. They are used to specific operating modes. They believe in certain philosophies. And all of these are hard to change.

My grandparents emigrated from Europe in the early 1900s. When they came over, they spoke the old language. So their children spoke the old language to communicate with them. But outside the house the children spoke English. Now the third generation can speak a few words of the old language, but they certainly can't converse in it.

It takes about three generations to change a culture. And you still have vestiges of the old. Now the time frame in a corporation is not that long, because a generation of management is shorter. But if you want to redirect the culture, I believe it will take ten to twenty years to be able to say, "We really have changed."

A culture tends to perpetuate itself. When you hire, you tend to pick somebody that looks very much like you and your boss look. He or she probably hired you for the same reason. You're compatible. The new person talks a certain way, comes from a certain educational background, and has certain outlooks that contribute to perpetuating the culture. One way the culture manifests itself as a barrier to change can be seen by observing a typical business cycle.

Most companies are formed around a product or technology idea. They then go into the manufacturing mode—making the product. But as competition surfaces, they suddenly have to become market oriented. However, the entrenched manufacturing culture can't really understand marketing. It's hard to change when you're staffed with people who are fluent only in the old country's language.

Take a look at our chemical industry. We've gone through some significant changes since the early sixties. At that time, when the industry was still almost in its infancy, it was almost irrelevant what you commercialized. If you wanted to grow, you just followed the formula: Build another plant; bring out another product—Somebody will buy it; somebody will find a use for it. In the late sixties and early seventies, the transition from a product/technology push to a market orientation started to occur. So true marketing organizations started to appear. Some companies made the transition very well, and some companies didn't make it at all.

Looking at culture issues, one chemical company that appears to have made significant changes for the 1980s and beyond is ICI. They are also an example of how leadership at the CEO level can effect the change. ICI executives apparently examined their portfolio during the 1970s and recognized many low-growth, commodity-oriented businesses in a world that was changing. Furthermore, the fastest-growing market for many of the advanced offerings was one in which they had participated little—the United States. So ICI did two key things. They built up their presence in the United States and changed their product line portfolio. The jury is still out, but they seem to be well positioned to be a major, worldwide player for the foreseeable future.

But this repositioning took a top-level commitment by ICI—a strong will and a long-term orientation. It didn't just happen a few years ago. It started long before then, and it is still happening. And the strategy seems firm and constant—not immovable, but constant, with the big strategic picture in place. From the observer's view, changes were evidenced by bold acquisition moves. For acquisitions that were strategically important to them, the industry and financial community initially said they paid too much. Whether they will ever see a return on that money, no one can say for sure. But they have certainly changed the corporation and its portfolio.

Internal developments were also part of the culture change, serving both to establish direction for what they should do strategically and to supplement the big moves made through acquisitions. At ICI it happened because of the visible leadership and commitment of the top guy, coupled with a rational strategy that was clearly understood and remained constant.

Culture change to spur creativity and innovation is in progress throughout much of American industry, the chemical industry included. Monsanto's and Kodak's pushes toward the life sciences are just two examples. Others include more acquisitions and partnering, internal venturing programs, and creative financing arrangements, as well as the incredible ongoing efforts for change under the banner of "quality," which is a lot less statistics and a lot more culture and operational philosophy than is generally recognized.

Risk Aversion

Another part of culture that explains why creativity does not start or innovation is not successful, is risk aversion. People are comfortable doing the things they're already doing. It takes an unusual person or a cataclysmic event to change. Risk aversion is pervasive. If the organization has a history of rewarding people who step out a little bit, then it promotes that type of behavior. On the other hand, if the organization immediately slaps someone on the wrist for stepping out a little bit—or for slipping a little bit while doing so—it will provoke a different behavior.

I'm not proposing that companies keep rewarding somebody who repeatedly steps out and makes mistakes. But there has to be some tolerance of failure, because it is going to happen. In fact, more aggressive organizations promote the belief that if you're not making mistakes, you're not taking enough risks.

I don't consider a gradual long-term decline in profitability, or growth stagnation, a cataclysmic event. But even going into a survival mode for a while requires creativity. It involves more than just universally and indiscriminately slashing costs. Certain critical functions have to be supported. There can be a lot of creativity in running a mature business—just as much as in trying to create something new.

But also look at other types of cataclysmic events; for example, a new technology coming along, like semiconductors in the early 1960s. When was the last time you saw a mechanical calculator? Some industry participants couldn't handle change. They tried what seemed to them to be a risk-aversion approach: to build a more efficient mechanical machine. It obviously didn't work. The new technology didn't *change* these companies—it *killed* them!

Lack of Perspective

Sometimes creativity doesn't start because of a tendency toward internal focus. The longer you look at yourself, the longer you kid yourself. You tend to put on blinders about what's happening in the outside world. You begin losing your perspective and objectivity entirely.

Many companies who say they are market oriented and customer focused, and who use all those wonderful words, really aren't. They are staying within their own comfort zones. Most organizations also maintain rather distinct internal functional barriers. For example, companies usually have job descriptions that employees abide by rigorously. The message is, "You're an R&D person and that's a marketing question, so don't be concerned with it; somebody in marketing will look at it."

Breaking down barriers that promote myopic behavior is a necessity for creativity and innovation, or you'll find you can only think about a little piece of something. You'll lose your "feel" for the bigger picture. And the narrower you become, the less creative you're going to be.

The holder of a Ph.D. is often driven to become narrower and narrower in his or her discipline. Yet many people think that a Ph.D. and creativity are synonymous. It's rare to get true creativity out of someone who is focused narrowly. So the tight job description leads to the "it's not my job" type of thinking. In many organizations this is a significant barrier.

Another barrier to creativity often cited is the lack of discretionary time. When you work for an organization, you're generally deemed to be fully employed. Fully employed means that if you're not visibly doing something during all your hours of employment—and usually beyond—then obviously you don't have enough to do. But generally, I categorize this as an excuse, not a real barrier. People who are creative will make time for themselves one way or another. So when people say, "I don't have the time to do such and such, so I can't be creative or get into new things," it's frequently a cop-out. If you're creative enough, you'll find the time.

From another perspective, however, truly dedicated managers will sometimes make sure you can't be creative. They'll pile onto you things that are really unnecessary, again with the theory that if you have your feet up on the desk, you're obviously not fully employed. But if the leadership and enabling environment are there, you will respond and feel motivated. If, however, somebody chops off your toe every time you stick it out, you'll stop quickly. Only an idiot would persist. But usually that "idiot" will persist in some other environment. And the former managers will probably say, "That person was such a radical; it's a good thing she left."

Lack of Hands-on Experience

Why do organizations seem to erect barriers to creativity? Companies often are organized to keep doing the things they normally do best, the things they're used to doing in order to serve yesterday's and today's businesses. But they're not necessarily the things that have to be done for future businesses. Most people don't understand what goes into the creation of new things. They might *say* they do, but precious few have genuinely done it themselves—that is, created something new. So there's a minimum of appreciation for what it takes: the time frame, effort, concentration, dedication, the ups and the downs, and all the rest.

Often a manager who is running an ongoing business is assigned the additional responsibility for starting new things. Unless that person is unusual, he almost always fails because the firefighting required by the current business takes precedence. So the resources that the individual puts in place to try to get new things going are redirected to helping the current business look better, rather than being used as they were intended to be. And this happens over a relatively short period of time. That's why so much R&D becomes customer service.

Over the years many companies have had what they call exploratory or long-term research. If this unit is not truly separated out and managed separately, it's soon doing short-term, customer-related work. Even the world-renowned Bell Laboratories almost fell into this trap just a few years back.

Many companies have held the traditional philosophy that a manager is a manager is a manager. I don't subscribe to it. Some people are good at starting things, some at growing things, some at maintaining things, and others at killing things. An individual might be able to do two of these well, but to be competent in all of them is highly unusual. Transforming a maintenance manager into a business development executive is difficult. Asking an entrepreneur to become a maintenance manager is likewise straining personality. So there are barriers that again go back to cultural issues—hiring people just like us. A maintenance manager tends to hire somebody who can also be a maintenance manager one day. You don't hire the maverick who has all these wonderful new ideas and wants to get something else started.

Leadership: most everything evolves from it—changing the culture, the people, the internal focus, the reward systems. Productive creativity revolves around leadership.

2

WHEN CREATIVITY STARTS BUT STOPS
Curses of Magic Ideas and Big Fallacies

Periodically, it seems, companies turn to creativity as the answer to their problems. And in reality, the answers provided can have momentous import and sometimes even can be the salvation of an executive or a company. More often than not, however, companies are nearly forced into their periodic love affair with creativity by unpleasant surprises from competitors, including enviable new products or services, a declining sales or profit curve, or the personal enthusiasm of a unique, high-level executive.

CREATIVITY'S SHAKY START

Most often the creative effort is a disorganized, shotgun foray on many fronts. The objective? To fan the elusive spark of creativity. And if fingers were not burned too badly in the last conflagration (or have healed into forgetfulness), the organization potentially can respond with vigor. However, because these creative efforts are usually poorly or totally unfocused, and there are no collective preagreed standards for evaluating the cacophonous output, meaningful actions seldom result.

One factor that contributes to the disappointing results is the widespread fallacy that coming up with innovative new products, services, or business growth opportunities is easy. Because most companies seldom do anything truly new, this naïveté is almost understandable. Some of the phrases we have heard reported by frustrated executives given the responsibility for business growth clearly support the premise that managers view the task as an easy one. For example,

"All we have to do is put someone on it."

"Just visit a trade show and you'll have enough ideas to keep you busy for a long time."

"Just get your salespeople to ask their customers for new product suggestions."

"Just get together some of your creative people and have a brainstorming session."

"Ask your ad agency to come up with new products; it's their job."

Some wag coined the phrase "Nothing difficult is ever easy." But getting creativity started is a lot easier than getting it focused on something productive, which, in turn, is easier than ultimately achieving a significant productive result.

Creativity can start for many reasons. However, keeping the spark glowing is not easy, and bringing successful (profitable) business opportunities to market is far from the capabilities of the inexperienced and naïve.

WHY CREATIVITY STOPS

One reason that most companies are not very successful in generating meaningful new products or business opportunities is they really haven't had a lot of practice. In most companies, *new* means an improvement or variation on an existing product or service. But another significant reason is the belief in the "magic idea" myth.

By definition, a magic idea is one that arrives full blown and

1. entails little or no risk;
2. requires little or no investment;

3. can be implemented almost immediately with little or no pain;
4. requires no changes in the key functional areas, that is, manufacturing, sales, and so on;
5. delivers instant profitable sales; and
6. generates a higher level of profits than any other undertaking in the company's history.

If these are the standards against which all mere mortal ideas are judged, none will receive top management's acceptance or generate enthusiastic support. Because only a few ideas ever achieve the status of magic, the merely solid ones are rejected.

Thus, the creative output that generated ordinary, hard-work ideas is not valued, and the individuals who contributed their very personal ideas feel disappointed, rejected, and frustrated. Now the fires of creativity return to a feeble spark, and the organization's enthusiasm for creativity ends up at a *lower* level, made worse by organizational inertia. Sometimes it seems that the only real issue is where management wants the new profits delivered.

Take our word for it, it's not that easy. Legions of frustrated business growth executives and hundreds of millions of dollars, if not billions, can attest to this fact.

Smoke Screens

Sometimes creativity only *looks* like it has started. Some organizations have an incredible capacity to create protective smoke screens. Here, creativity is represented by furious activity that somehow never produces any meaningful results. In fact, the real objective is not to produce any disturbing results but to give the *appearance* of addressing the right issues.

This situation often occurs when a powerful, high-level executive takes the position that something must be done about new products or business opportunities and proclaims this loudly throughout the organization. However, this same individual totally abandons any responsibility for or interest in the quest and provides no focus for the search efforts.

One giant corporation we know well had a high-level professional staff approaching a dozen well-paid individuals supported by another few dozen appropriate personnel. The managers of this new business development organization worked diligently to generate what ultimately became four large loose-leaf binders of ideas that had been examined and either rejected or kept for further consideration. The net result of nearly three years of work was that one small acquisition was made, but it was disposed within a year. During this period, if anyone had asked a top executive whether he or she was doing anything about new products or business growth, the answer would have been a resounding yes. But the effort was destined to failure because it had no real emotional support, focus, or commitment from the management. So one reason that creativity stops is that it never really starts—it only appears to have started.

Overprotectiveness toward Ideas

Creativity sometimes stops because the originator of the idea refuses to submit his precious infant idea to running the gauntlet, which has become traditional in the culture of the organization. He would rather shelve the idea safely and securely in the hopes that future times and management attitudes will be more receptive than subject it and himself to the embarrassment or trauma of a hostile review by others who have little or no understanding or sympathy for what goes into the creation and presentation of a new idea. Hence, potentially profitable opportunities languish on the shelf—usually forever. Occasionally, some are discovered and taken off by other companies whose leaders recognize their merit and build successful businesses around them.

We were involved in exactly that situation in a growth program for a Finnish company, Orion OY, operating in the medical diagnostics market. A technology had been developed by a large American medical products company. After a few feeble attempts to move the product system into commercialization, it was shelved indefinitely. There it was identified, as a result of the highly vertical networking that occurs on a well-focused and -targeted growth program, and purchased by Orion. The Orion staff created a company around the new system for automatically and rapidly monitoring and detecting bacterial growth. The company, Bactomatic, created a successful business, which ultimately—for a variety of reasons unrelated to the product line itself—was sold to McDonnell Douglas, where it is currently housed.

Although the parent business was not conducive to the successful marketing of this idea, the inventor or inventors could only be disappointed to see their cherished offspring sold at auction. These situations may be inevitable, but they still exact their toll on the morale and motivation underlying creative activity in an organization.

Too Little or Too Much Risk Taking

Why do young Democrats often become middle-aged Republicans? Because they have something to *lose!* Revolutions and risk taking are not the province of the establishment; they are the priorities of groups that have nothing to lose. So we propose that creativity often dies because the founders and management begin to have something to lose.

Companies are no different from people because companies *are* people. We don't have to look far in our personal lives to find that most mature individuals resist change. It's the exceptional person who still seeks change by middle age or beyond. Often, older people not only resist change, they *hate* it. The same usually applies to organizations.

Certain characteristics set the entrepreneurial company apart from the large, mature company. Whereas employees of large organizations often complain of bureaucracy and inertia, those in small companies often have an undersupply and too little structure. Consequently, they may be overeager to change and try something new.

Whereas a large, bureaucratic, mature company resists change at any price, the smaller entrepreneurial company or group has no inoculum against too much change, which can dissipate resources and energies. Again, we encounter the necessity and intrinsic value of having a focus and a clear vision—even in a small startup.

Ironically, small, creative companies often become bureaucratic and uncreative as a consequence of achieving the success for which they worked so hard. They then reject new ideas and become risk averse. The resulting inertia and stagnation produce the next generation of entrepreneurial spin-offs, and the cycle starts all over again.

Ways of dealing with this perennial problem of bureaucratic rigidity resulting from success are evident at W. L. Gore & Associates. Founder Bill Gore, much to his credit, decided to keep his radically informal lattice organization small—at the most, 200 people per unit. Upon approaching this size, an operation is downsized into two or more entities, thus keeping the informality, excellent communication, and intimacy inherent in small size. Also, the company is notorious for its lack of titles. Everyone in the organization at any level carries the title of associate.

RapidPurge Corporation, an INNOTECH subsidiary, specifically states in its mission statement, "While committed to growth, the company will accommodate expansion by creating stand-alone profit centers in order to maintain working units of less than 100 people, thus preserving the cohesiveness and teamwork of a small, highly-motivated group working for the betterment of RapidPurge . . . and each other."

Peer Group Pressure

Another reason creativity dies is peer group pressure. Individuals begin to think, If *he* fails, he'll look bad and I'll get ahead.

The message then is, Don't make a mistake your peers could exploit.

Interestingly, years ago an executive with General Mills showed us a curve that had been developed after doing research on risk taking in the organization. The curve was a perfect *U*. The top of the graph represented high risk taking and the base, low. The researchers found that the left side of the *U*—high risk taking—described entry-level employees. They had little equity or personal stakes in the organization and, consequently, felt they had little or nothing to lose.

The right side of the *U*, also high risk taking, described the top management—chairman, chief executive officer, and chief operating officer. These people were secure in their success and achievements and consequently were more inner-directed. So they too ranked high in risk taking.

This leaves us with the bottom of the curve—the lowest risk taking. Here was an arena peopled by middle management. These folks had a large career investment in the organization, essentially no security, lots of peer group pressure and competition, and a lot to loose.

LACK OF A CHAMPION

One key reason why creativity stops is that no champion is available to move a new product into commercial reality. The central importance of the champion cannot be overrated. Therefore, the ability to find and enlist the right champions also cannot be overrated.

Many factors affect the identification and encouragement of champions. Even if we recognize the value of finding a superior individual to act as a champion, we might find very few superior individuals amid many solid performers. Unfortunately, the 80:20 rule probably applies here: 80 percent of the true contributions in an organization come from 20 percent of the individuals.

If we take away the failure potential and provide secure safety nets for the champion, we'll probably get more than our share of solid performers with an "intellectual interest"—given the fact that there is no downside in the undertaking. With such a scenario several individuals will probably be willing to take the nonrisk. However, if the safety net is not there, then clearly the upside of success must be terrific to attract candidates. An individual must feel that he or she can become a lot better off after the success occurs.

Career Path Problems

It seems fairly reasonable and logical that if a company's managers are investing in the organization's future survival and growth, they should staff creative projects with their best and brightest. Yet they often do this reluctantly because these folks are so valuable and essential in other important or critical areas. The boss then may be reluctant to volunteer them for a high-risk assignment that takes them away from their already invaluable contribution.

From the other point of view, the best and the brightest are on a fast career track. If these types of people sense that the downside is more significant than the upside, they will resist becoming involved with the venture because of the potential loss of their fast track. The consequence is that superior talent won't sign on for a new venture. To fix this problem, companies must rethink their compensation schemes in order to create incentives for success that will make the chase worthwhile.

These career-related problems surfaced on a venture program for a leading packaged goods company. Top operating management was asked to provide some good people for the new venture program. They didn't, and those they did send were already career flawed. No one was optimistic about their ability to perform in the challenging venture arena. (This, in fact, is often not the case, because "career-flawed" individuals may view the challenge of a new venture as the vehicle to repair the damage to their career and reemerge at the top.) After top management was pressured to send higher-quality people, the problem surfaced: these people did not want to become involved with the high risk of a venture.

A core principle of venturing was violated here—that the venturist must be self-selected. He or she must want to accept the challenges of moving an idea through the birth pains of commercialization. Successful venturists are seldom apppointed. However, if they are, the downside must be nearly eliminated and the upside made extremely attractive. If not, the venturist will prove that the venture has no merit and hurry back to his or her preexisting situation.

The Potential for Punishment

Unfortunately, in many companies the potential for punishment of an individual who pursues a creative enterprise and fails is high. So creativity may stop because the word is out that this is the operating culture. Some companies seem to have a "primal" code that deals with almost everything in terms of black or white. Therefore, success is white and failure is black. If an organization's leaders want to avoid unintentionally emasculating their company's creative and business development efforts, they must become far more sophisticated in determining and establishing what a failure means before individuals connected with one are labeled failures.

What does *failure* mean? Answering this question in a far more sophisticated way than black or white has a critical bearing on champions—creative leaders—potential champions, and ultimately the culture of the organization. If the champion of an idea was truly a major component of the failure because of inaction, lack of commitment, lack of intelligence, or poor leadership, any of these would be legitimate reasons for pointing a finger at that person. However, normally this individual is motivated to succeed and work diligently and intelligently in pursuit of a goal. Therefore, in the great majority of cases in which an attempt to bring a seemingly promising idea to commercialization fails, the root causes lie beyond the champion, and he or she should not be rejected or punished.

Creativity Disincentive Programs

All too often companies have incentive systems that work against even experimenting with the new. We were intimately involved in a growth program for a major paper company. The objective of the program was to find new applications and market opportunities for a rather unique product. This happened, and upon its conclusion, the program was judged successful.

However, when attempts to get some of the concepts prototyped met with strong resistance from the plant operating manager, the fact surfaced that he and his management team received strong incentives to keep the machines running at maximum output. To stop and modify the equipment in order to run material for prototyping and experimenting with new products would have taken a large personal sacrifice by the production management group.

They weren't prepared to do this, nor was management ready to change the compensation system. So we all confronted the dichotomous thinking of top management, who wanted new products in order to achieve a meaningful return on a significant investment, and operating management, who could not change the system to allow the products to happen.

We have run into many such creativity and risk-taking disincentive programs, not only in manufacturing but more broadly in marketing, sales, and even at the top management level. The ultimate top-management disincentive program is the "tyranny of earnings-per-share management." Given that creativity leads to risk taking, which leads, in turn, to change, new products, risk, and long development times, doing something new is almost out of the question if it requires any of these.

Midcourse "Corrections"

Sometimes a dedicated and effective program is launched with seemingly everything going for it. Criteria have been established, promising opportunity areas found, and specific implementation vehicles identified for moving the company into the new possibilities. At this point, the Klaxon horn sounds loudly and the CEO's voice comes down into the engine room with the order, "Reverse engines!"

Unfortunately, many times the reasons are as valid as spotting an iceberg dead ahead: raiders strike, profits and funds evaporate, or someone makes valid strategic decisions about refocusing on or away from a core business. The sad surprises of life that affect us as individuals do not spare even well-managed corporations.

So another reason creativity stops is that, given a unique set of unexpected circumstances, it truly has to. Whatever the reasons, though, the event still has severely debilitating emotional impact on the individuals who were pursuing what clearly appeared to be a rational strategy when it was launched.

A few examples come to mind. In the first, a large chemical and materials company was involved in a growth program that had as its specific objective finding an acquisition that would broaden and supplement the business base of a division. Almost to the day when the management group identified the perfect acquisition and announced their readiness to go after it, the chairman of the corporation promulgated a policy statement declaring that for at least an interim period of a few years, no further acquisitions would be made.

In another case, a leading tobacco company, already diversified into a number of nontobacco areas, was ready to take its packaging division and move it more vertically into some promising and profitable ventures in the medical arena. Again, at the eleventh hour, the chairman addressed a group of security analysts and said that the focus of the company from that instant on would be to stay close to its core businesses and not move into any new areas.

Neither decision can be viewed as irrational or erratic, but each came as a hard blow to a highly motivated and creative management team.

Musical Chairs Management

People in the trenches attempting to be creative and identify new growth opportunities are all too frequently subject to the winds blown by revolving top management. One CEO may state firmly that the organization has to become more creative and risk-taking, so all the organizational gears are set in that direction and are smoothly meshing and producing the desired output. Enter, stage left, a new CEO. She declares, "We have some real short-term problems, so unfortunately, we don't have time for all this creativity stuff."

Because generating and developing new business opportunities are not overnight activities, and because executives tend to change positions frequently while those activities are under way, it's understandable that growth processes and CEOs often get out of synch. Thus, a well-conceived and -implemented new business development effort is frequently aborted somewhere along the way by a new executive who has a different strategy for the solution of an organization's problems and a different vision of how to shape a viable future. The problem of taking a longer-range view is one that will rear its ugly head several times during our discussions on why creativity has extreme difficulty bearing fruit in certain kinds of organizations.

The Real Decision Makers Are Not Involved

Perhaps aided and abetted by their realization of a lack of knowledge regarding creativity, many top executives simply relegate their responsibilities to others and remain at arm's length. This lack of visible support and direction certainly doesn't motivate those charged with the responsibility. More important, it virtually insures that the resulting output will never be commercialized because it does not fit the "vision" of the top manager or managers who will ultimately be charged with committing funds and saying yes or no.

We always counsel executives who do not control the purse strings or the final decision about pursuing significant growth activities to take the criteria—which represent their vision—to those who do have the final say. These are the people who should be exposed to them eventually if any significant amounts of time or money will be invested. Their support must be gained as early as possible to prevent unpleasant surprises after a lot of hard work and emotional commitment are rejected.

Overoptimism and Unrealistic Goals

We've all heard the expression "talk is cheap." Sincere, well-intentioned management groups can become most ambitious when discussing their growth goals. Sometimes diligent, creative efforts to translate these goals into realistic and promising opportunities pay off. However, when suddenly confronted by an opportunity that will require a large investment, many managers get cold feet. It was easy to laugh and joke about the tiger when he was not in sight. But now that his tail is in your hands the consequences can be imagined all too vividly. This factor is probably one of the most troublesome in attempting to establish realistic criteria for a growth program.

One way of imposing reality on out-of-control ambitions is to find out what investment levels applied in earlier instances. A management group can glibly state that they want a major new opportunity to yield profits in the commercial marketplace within a year. When asked how long it took the last one to reach this stage, they may find that the answer is five to seven years.

When specifically asked how much they would be willing to invest to realize this significant new growth opportunity, managers often say, "We'll put whatever it takes into the right idea." This reply begs the question: "right idea" really means "magic idea." So while executives avow their willingness to invest whatever it takes, they are less willing to invest the first few thousand dollars to find out if one or more specific ideas could ever be the right idea.

Given that companies normally have mechanisms for spending funds, the problem is often not one of reluctance to commit the funds but rather the bureaucratic difficulty of dealing with risk monies versus investments. We contend it is easier to invest $20 million in building a plant when you can take calculations out to at least the second decimal place and you have built others like it before. It's far more difficult to risk $50,000 for an uncertain undertaking that could get nixed.

Such decision-making bias has forced us to develop the concept of "get-smart money." This is money earmarked and set aside at the beginning of a business growth program to be accessed far more simply and easily than typical financial requisitions. A company should think of it as prefinal decision-making research. Such money limits the possible losses before a serious decision is made about investing significant funds to bring a concept to commercial reality.

So we have another reason why creativity stops: its efforts have resulted in something far beyond the appetite of the sponsoring organization.

Creativity Is Hard Work

Any creative undertaking holds the potential for disappointment and failure. This fact raises the level of intensity, which can become extremely draining emotionally. Creativity can burn people out—unless out of self-preservation, they simply walk away before burning out. Being creative takes far more energy than operating in areas that are familiar and safe. If habit is the repetition of a proven successful solution, creative thinking—constantly exploring the new—is the antithesis of habit. The familiar is easy, the unfamiliar is strange, if not downright scary. So managers should understand not only that creative people can be difficult to deal with but also that creativity involves hard work and is difficult to sustain.

ANOTHER VIEW FROM THE REAL WORLD

Derwyn Phillips

Derwyn Phillips is vice-chairman of the Gillette Company, with operating responsibility for the North Atlantic region, which includes the company's activities in the United States, Europe, and Canada.

He first became involved with INNOTECH's Planned Growth process in the early 1980s on a range of activities, starting with generating corporate criteria.

Mr. Phillips was the prime mover on a successful new venture program that had to be aborted when large expenditures of capital were required to respond to several takeover attempts. In the process of buying up about one-third of its shares, the company decided that it could no longer fund ventures outside its core businesses.

I would say that we succeeded in venturing into three new businesses where our Gillette entrepreneurs did learn the business, did create a viable enterprise, and given sufficient funding and patience, I'm convinced would have created business success.

WHAT ARE SOME OF THE IMPORTANT LEARNING EXPERIENCES?

Need for Top-Management Support

Risk programs into new business areas, regardless of their size, cannot get off the ground in a large company without top management support. We succeeded in getting senior operating management to support the idea that we should try some dramatically different things which might give us the potential for accelerated growth in the 1990s. That was a critical element— getting the key operating managers supporting the idea that we ought to develop some longer-range ideas on new business areas that we could fund. Often the reason new ideas fail is that the organization doesn't support them with the kind of total commitment they demand. So, if you can get the right management level to sponsor, to point the way, to support a concept, this support creates a "potential for heroes" down in the organization. To use the military analogy, the second lieutenant *knows* he can be a hero because all the top brass are pointing at this very special hill. One of the most important pieces of the fabric in any company's culture is that the organization performs up to the level it thinks management expects. So if management visibly expects excellence and creativity in the area of new opportunities, new growth, and innovation, that's what it's likely to get. It comes down to expectations. It's interesting to observe that a large percentage of companies have incentive programs designed to get the organization to perform toward certain objectives. I don't believe it's necessarily the incentive itself that produces the result. Rather, it's the process of making clear to the organization what the people at the top of the company expect. The incentive may be relatively unimportant. In many companies people are confused as to what the desired mission really is. That's why so many people today are talking about vision, mission, and values. The process is answering the questions, What is expected of me? What are the standards of performance that we think are important? That's what mission and values are all about. So I suggest that visible and total support from the top is essential for success.

Sponsors and Champions

Another key component in any program to do something new is a high-level "sponsor" to whom people look with respect. I think this is critical. Somebody has to provide the leadership on each project, or you won't generate much that is new. That's really where it all starts, because that person has to persuade the other key management players in the organization that "this is a good idea" and that "this is a solid plan." Otherwise, it will fail. Beyond the sponsor, however, you need the champions—the venturers themselves, the people who will make it happen day by day. I suspect that this area may be one of the biggest problems with entrepreneurship in a large company.

Once again, we're back to the idea of organizational expectations. The organization tends to tell the people (generally through "body movement") what the logical career paths are, and this becomes an important part of the environment and culture. Thus, every young person that comes into the management stream looks and sees the signals and says, "Oh, there's the career path to the top of this company." When you attempt to install an entrepreneurial concept to start a new business—which demands dramatically higher risk in that same organization—you suddenly run out of potential entrepreneurs. It's because the exceptional person who respects the fact that he or she is exceptional chooses to believe that he or she has the resources to make it up the hierarchy without becoming involved in this high-risk entrepreneurial game. Before we figured this out, we discovered to our surprise that we did not have a long line of exceptional people wanting to rush off and take the high risks of becoming entrepreneurs. Bottom line: Many young people feel that they don't need to risk failure. Also, they're cautious because they doubt that the organization will give them permission to fail.

As a consequence, when we decided that we had to wind our venturing activities down, we made it a priority to see that all our entrepreneurs obtained important jobs in the core business units. I believe that it's imperative to provide the kind of safety net that allows the entrepreneurs to "go home again" if the venture is shut down for any reason. If you ever want to start venturing again, have a track record that demonstrates that champions end up with solid challenges and opportunities when they come out of the entrepreneurial game and back into the mainstream.

Patience and the Long-range View

I suspect that most large companies who begin new ventures grossly underestimate the difficult hurdles that the venturer must cross in putting together the details of the business plan. Also, managements generally delude themselves into expecting positive cash flow far too quickly. You had better have a large supply of patience pills, because there is plenty of pain in the process, and positive people generally commit themselves to performance objectives that are too stringent. My guess is that, on average, startups probably need a five- to seven-year window for positive cash flow—patience.

So We Had to Shut Down

Because of a number of activities we might lump under the title "the new Wall Street," many companies have been forced to come back to, and focus all their efforts on, strengthening their core businesses. And this has really caused a narrowing of their diversification activities to those that fit their core business areas, not entirely new businesses. We've seen a lot of that during the last few years, and we'll see more in the future. It's certainly a key factor in our particular case.

From late 1986 through early 1988 our company was under direct attack from both takeover attempts and proposals to sell or break up the company. In the process of maintaining independence as the best way to maximize shareholder value, we created significant debt through share buyback programs. More debt means fewer resources to spread and increased pressure to make more tradeoffs. We came to the conclusion that we could not continue to fund our new ventures program. Each demanded substantial future funding, and we concluded it was imperative that we refocus all resources on our core businesses. We sold off our interests in these three venture areas.

WHAT WOULD WE DO DIFFERENTLY
IF WE WERE TO BEGIN AGAIN?

In retrospect, I believe that our overall program would have been even more successful had we demanded in our criteria that we remain closer to one of our principal corporate strategies. Gillette is a federation of a half dozen relatively closely related businesses—personal care and personal use products. A key corporate strategy has been to focus on like businesses that can share functional resources and services and that have common retail customers.

We have resource sharing across our businesses of probably a dozen human and functional resource areas. The closer the businesses in terms of customers, the greater the resource sharing. One obvious example is the distribution function. Through one organization we distribute the majority of the products that we sell in most major developed areas of the world. As a second example, we have a common media-buying operation so that we control the buying of advertising through one central organization. Presumably, all of these central services contribute added value to the sharing units, and those units receive services at lower cost than they would if they did it themselves—and get better quality. If that is not valid and if we can't support the case for sharing, we shouldn't be doing it. We ought to be adding value beyond what the business units can get on their own and doing it at a lower cost.

Now with that as background, let's look at our 1980s venturing effort. Much of it took us beyond this strategy, that is, the number of common facilities that could be shared by some of the business areas we ventured into was very low. So, in effect, we were stepping outside a basic strategy and caused a certain amount of discomfort in the more "conservative" zones of the culture. Next time out I'd be inclined to make this at least a desirable criterion and probably a must.

One of the fundamental issues that any company has to come to grips with today is the question of whether or not it should risk stepping outside of its existing areas of business expertise, and whether it should focus only on creating greatness in its core business areas. I judge that the answer depends on how high your real growth target is and the level you believe you can deliver from your core businesses. I'm convinced that regardless of how big your brand shares are—regardless of how well you are doing— you can always improve your performance in your core businesses. There are very few truly mature businesses. Maturity seems to develop in the minds of managers when creativity dries up. The creative organization is the one that can grow share in the markets others describe as mature. So, I subscribe to the argument that you should make certain that you have an established competitive advantage and organizational excellence in your core business or businesses before you even think about venturing beyond. You'd better be the best there is in your core business before you look beyond, and the people in your organization had better understand that that's always the first priority. In any event, somewhere, sometime, somehow you have to make the gut decision: Can you afford to, and can you risk a step out culturally, financially, or emotionally?

The Need for Real Growth

Another aspect to consider is that while you may be "growing" in the businesses you're in, are you growing fast enough? I'm really convinced that as time passes, shareholders will put much more emphasis on real growth in balance with EPS [earnings per share] growth. Many companies have lived off improvements in productibity in recent years. Leaner organizational structures have been achieved through various restructuring efforts that have squeezed improved productivity from existing resources. Consequently, earnings per share have been developing nicely, but not from real growth, not from the truly new—or, at least, not enough from the truly new.

I conclude that in striving for high sustained profitable growth, every organization should have a "skunk works"* in place which has the total support of top management and which is reaching into the future to isolate new consumer wants and new patterns of distribution which can lead to strategic change or an entirely new business opportunity.

*A low-budget facility operating on almost no money in order to get new products developed and started.

3

WHERE CREATIVITY STARTS (OR RESTARTS) AND FLOURISHES
Characteristics of a Supportive Culture

A large mural-like sign in the foyer of INNOTECH's offices in Connecticut says "Business Is the Commercialization of an Idea." Companies are almost always *born* into a creative ambience. A business starts as an idea in the mind of the entrepreneur or founding group. Their business concept can be innovative—that is, new to the world—or it can be a new company to exploit an existing idea. There are fundamental similarities between the two; the differences are only those of degree.

Perhaps one way of putting new product or business development into perspective is to view a company as a bucket with a hole in it. The hole can vary in size, and the rate of leakage will depend on the size of the hole. The hole can come from the market in which the organization functions, be a consequence of where on the product life cycle the company's business lies, or be the conscious sloughing off of some percentage of its existing business. That's the "rate of leakage."

Clearly, then, for an organization to survive there must be a flow of new ideas and products into the top of the bucket that at least meets the rate of leakage. That's why it is critical to take a realistic view of attempts to generate new business and recognize that while we can't win them all, we'd better keep trying.

HOW TO KEEP CREATIVITY GOING

Keeping any good thing going such as a culture supportive of creativity takes work—even when an organization has a genuine commitment to it. This "work" can be nothing more sophisticated than periodic reminders of this commitment—and the anticipated benefits that motivated it. Sometimes it's not what you *know*, but what you *remember* to do. Reminders of having this commitment can show up in many appropriate vehicles, from memos to rewards.

Recognize the Value of Risk

Creativity and risk are inseparable, so the element of risk is typically highest in the entrepreneurial startup of an innovative idea. However, risks exist even in an organization designed to exploit an established idea. In the latter, these risks include people relationships, acceptance of the new entity in the marketplace, and many times the load of carrying the requisite financing. We're sure that those of you who have been in this situation can think of several more. Our point, then, is that doing *anything* new entails some degree of creativity and, consequently, risk.

ENCOURAGE VISION AND LEADERSHIP

Because creativity always entails risk and thinking creatively is hard work, organizations can only keep creativity going once it starts by being visibly successful at using creativity and by having people share in the rewards of these successes. But this elusive thing called success, especially in the arena of creativity as applied to new products and business opportunities, is heavily dependent on a management group strong enough to make decisions about the future, establish criteria (which automatically exclude more than they allow through), and promulgate all the above in a mission or vision statement that focuses, motivates, and inspires. And all of this cannot occur in an organization that is simplistic in its binary judgments of success or failure.

Keeping a group heading in a creative direction with momentum requires some unique leadership skills. People with these skills typically exhibit enthusiasm, commitment, vision, a sense of humor, and a heavy dose of the type of positive attitude that flowed from such classic leaders and motivators as Knute Rockne or Vince Lombardi. This does not necessarily imply a rah-rah style of leadership, because effective leaders can be found covering the entire range of personality types from quiet and unassuming . . . to the bombastic. These styles are merely the "clothing" in which the other leadership characteristics come through.

ELIMINATE CREATIVITY STOPPERS

To foster creativity you must eliminate the creativity stoppers discussed in Chapter 2 and try to find others that may be unique to your organization. One might be that, so far, the thinking has been to assign champions on a part-time basis—at least until the opportunity has proven itself viable. This can be a Catch 22 situation, because without sufficient champion time, the effort can be inadequate or too slow. The first management commitment that must be made, then, is to free up all or most of an individual's time to allow a fair first-step effort to be taken.

Fostering creativity is hard and can be emotionally draining, and individuals can burn out or get tired of the level of intensity it requires. Many organizations have recognized this withering effect and have tried to introduce components that will provide some fun and be revitalizing. One common tool is trips to exciting resorts or conference centers where creative work consumes only a portion of the day and the remainder is left for play.

Although recreation is not intrinsically necessary to the creative process, it clearly enhances interest in, and the value ascribed to, being creative. Also, when surrounded by familiar stimuli in the company's boardroom or other regular meeting site, people have much more difficulty thinking in new, creative ways. A change of scenery helps and the newness of the facility brings a heightened level of excitement and "electricity" to the creative tasks.

Don't Overrate Creativity

Creativity itself is not enough to move an organization successfully into new, profitable growth opportunities. In fact, without a strong management providing a clear focus, creativity can soon become a giant liability. Some individuals are "pathologically" creative. They constantly "invent" items that have no relevance or value and then sacrifice their families and fortunes in the pursuit of their "can't miss" electric paw warmers for Siamese cats.

We've met a lot of these poor souls. They are compulsive about being creative and can never bring anything into focus, closure, or reality. This type of individual acting like a loose cannon in an organization can create such a bad example that others "turn off" on the whole area of creativity.

So the ability to be creative when appropriate needs to be coupled with the ability to turn off creativity and focus on reality. However, even this rational type of creativity cannot be tolerated in a hostile environment. So some exceptionally bright and rationally creative people find themselves fairly early in their careers being shunted off into staff jobs at the second or third level where they will not prove too troublesome. All of this seems to be calling into focus the need to understand creativity, use it properly, and establish the culture and set up the mechanisms whereby it can truly be a valuable tool in the pursuit of rational growth and survival opportunities.

Offer Financial Incentives

We believe that financial incentives are primarily of value for the spouse and children of the venturist. Most true entrepreneurs are working for ego fulfillment and freedom (even though they rationalize that they are doing it for the family). Support from the family is crucial, because the venturist will typically give up the quest if the family feels threatened by potential losses. So the psychological value of financial incentives is a big plus. However, deciding how best to offer such incentives is no easy task.

The problem? How do you reward the other people in the organization who are working just as hard and creatively in support of the core business? In this particular situation we've provided no answers but merely identified the need and the challenge.

RESTARTING CREATIVITY

For a variety of reasons creativity may die—or be killed—and need to be restarted. Managers face unique challenges in rekindling creativity, because the ideas that creativity has produced are the "babies" of each individual who created them. When an idea is "born" in the mind of an individual, it is an intensely personal event. When the organization, for whatever reason, has a number of individuals whose babies have been killed, the culture is full of trauma that is not easy to overcome. As in any personal loss, it takes time, and there seldom are any quick fixes.

Tolerating Small Risks

How can we restart creativity? If a culture has become completely impervious to new ideas, one strategy that could help is to communicate the willingness to take small risks in attempting to do something new—perhaps even by publicly rewarding rational, small failures.

One of our clients, a leading chemical giant, launched an internal venturing program. The managers made clear that if some of the raw ideas for ventures proved not to be viable, the venturist or venture team would be rewarded for *killing* a non-viable venture. Such a "killing" then became a positive, rather than a negative, event. Thus, shooting a bad idea can make one a hero if the action is viewed as rational and is supported by good information. This approach certainly contrasts with the typical one of shooting the messenger who bears bad news. And getting bad news early is far better than getting it late.

Rebounding from Creativity Deprivation

Ironically, some highly creative organizations result as a reaction to having been very uncreative for a long time. A notable example comes to mind of a medium-size company in Pennsylvania manufacturing a line of simple mechanical products. After extensive "selling" (actually, more like *pleading*) by the members of the management group, headed by the vice-president of R&D, the elderly chairman reluctantly agreed to consider pursuing a diversification program that would move the company slightly away from its monopolistic core business and search for new growth opportunities. The organization had been consistently profitable but had showed no meaningful growth for several years. Clearly, members of the management team were frustrated and wanted to do *something.* So the program began.

Group meetings were an embarrassment to everyone because of the attitude and behavior of the soon-to-retire chairman, a tyrant who rode roughshod over the opinions and feelings of his management group. He totally dominated the meetings and superimposed so much negativity and ill will on everything and everyone that it became apparent this was a no-win situation for all involved. *Nothing* resulted directly from the exercise.

Not too long afterwards, the chairman was forced into an even earlier retirement for health reasons and was replaced with an executive from the other end of the spectrum. This laissez-faire CEO produced such a refreshing change in the climate that creativity *exploded.* No other changes were needed. People finally were free to pursue new ideas and opportunities without the intense fear of failure that had existed for years, and they did so with gusto. Fortunately, they had learned the value of criteria, so their efforts were well focused and highly productive. To this day, five years later, they still report a high level of creative productivity, many new product successes, and significant, highly profitable growth.

Eliminating the Fear of Failure

If creativity and risk taking existed in a company's early years but then died out, we need to consider how to restart it—how to get it back. First, we suggest one strategy that should underlie all our efforts: *eliminate the fear of failure!*

Ironically, it is exactly this fear that leads to most big failures, for we have found that the best way to make a *big mistake* is to try not to make any mistake at all. So the fear of failure leads to a dominating concern about making mistakes—which leads to bigger mistakes. Why? How?

Eliminating the possibility of a mistake often takes significant money and time for all the research, checks, and rechecks—ultimately producing information to the "third decimal point." However, the moment of truth—the time we find out what the mistakes are—is when we actually *do* something, that is, manufacture, provide the service, or bring the offering to market. Discovering the mistake at this point is usually too late. All the money and time that went into mistake prevention is lost, and the window of opportunity that we were attempting to exploit may well have closed.

Although it may sound facetious, the solution is to *make your mistake as fast as possible.* How? Whenever possible, make small, non-company/life/career-threatening mistakes. Fast mistakes are often small ones. To do this, however, you may need to reconsider, or reframe, your concept of a mistake.

An interesting example of reframing the way we look at something is to explore the difference between a *mistake* (an emotional, bad word) and *feedback* (an intelligent, good word). What is the fundamental difference? Size. Clearly, if millions of dollars are lost, that's a mistake; if thousands of dollars are lost, that's feedback. So the fear of making mistakes inevitably leads to big mistakes.

Creativity flourishes in an ambience which recognizes that doing something new may result in mistakes and failures. In other words, if you try something new, the possible outcomes are that you can either succeed or *learn. Learning* is a much better word than *failing.* If you don't try something new, neither benefit—succeeding or learning—can result.

Interestingly, the news emerged recently that according to some psychological studies, entrepreneurs report never taking risks! They are so totally confident of their ideas and abilities and so certain of a positive outcome that they see success as inevitable. Therefore, what would appear to an outsider as an enormous risk is to an entrepreneur no perceived risk at all.

THE BLESSINGS AND BENEFITS
OF RISK TAKING

Where there is support of limited, rational risks, creativity can be expected to exist and productively serve the organization, and many benefits will accrue to the working environment in general. Bureaucracy and politics flourish when the people in an organization have lost sight of its goals and their own.

When goals are paramount, politics takes second place and efforts are directed toward worthwhile accomplishments supported by the group. People *enjoy* their work! The culture becomes dynamic and interesting. With a good place to work, it is easy to recruit new talent that can perpetuate the momentum of success. We all know that success breeds success. This kind of organization gives us pride in being affiliated with it.

Such pride is clearly the feeling that emerges from talking to any of the associates at Gore. The 3M Company is viewed by many as the paragon when it comes to new products in a creative culture. Being part of a winning team is a source of great pride and reinforces the attributes that led to winning in the first place. Other blessings and benefits are that survival is more assured because the business and its future are not based solely on today's products or services.

ANOTHER VIEW FROM THE REAL WORLD

Cees Van Rij

As development manager for the New Business Group at AKZO, Cees Van Rij has been the prime mover on many new product development, innovation, and creativity programs within the fibers and polymers division of AKZO for many years. AKZO is a Dutch-based, leading international chemical company. As you will learn from the following, "Case" has a passion for really understanding creativity—and its interrelationship with a company's culture—at the most fundamental level, and he is writing a book on the subject.

Creativity Is Still the Same

I approach the subject of where creativity starts and flourishes by using a series of stories—some allegorical—and a few business examples from my career at AKZO.

Sometimes "answers" have more staying power and value when we have to work a bit to get them, rather than have them handed to us. My orientation is to go after the *fundamentals* of creativity, innovation, and human psychology as they relate to dealing with creative people in a business environment.

To understand how to deal with highly creative people, let's start by going back and looking at our ancestors some 20,000 years ago. At that time, people had exactly the same faces, the same bodies, and the same brain volume that we have today. We know a great deal about them and the physical conditions they lived under. It must have been a horrible time. They couldn't fly like birds or run as fast as animals. They could hardly protect themselves. And their children couldn't walk at all until they were well over a year old! The one special thing they did have was a tremendously overgrown brain.

Animals living in groups have a leader, a second in command, a third, and so on. The only difference between these animals is their level within the group. When you look at people 20,000 years ago, you find they also have these leadership levels. But they have another thing—specialization, that is, there are leaders, fighters, protectors, care givers, clever ones. You also have individuals that are not of much use. They do a lot of things like have fun, run around, play, and act foolishly. But, when it comes to some specific events, they suddenly become quite useful. These events are the out of the ordinary—the problems and dangers: saber-toothed tigers, floods, difficulties in finding food, fire, and water, and so on. At times when something has to be done to get the tribe out of trouble, all of a sudden these special people—these normally useless people—prove to be essential. Today we call these people creative.

Every ability or attitude or behavior you find in people today you can find in these people of 20,000 years ago. And so it is with creativity. Creative people today find their ancestors in the creative people of 20,000 years ago. So, many of our questions today about dealing with creative people in companies can be answered by exploring and truly understanding these creative people. Because there's no difference.

Creative People Tend to Be . . .

There are two things that I think are vital. First, many studies show that naturally creative people usually are action oriented. We could also use the words *assertive*, or even *aggressive*, to describe them—not the "looking for a fight" variety of aggression, but the positive tendency to jump forward when something is needed, being there when something happens.

Studies show that creative people are doers. They are active and always prepared for anything they can do to release the pressure that comes from inside, driving them to realize what their creativity can produce. This means that if I *truly* want creativity in an organization, I have to deal with people who are not only creative but who are also, to a certain extent, action oriented, assertive, and even "aggressive."

The consequences of these personality characteristics are important, and we will discuss these further. The second thing I want to discuss is that creativity is not a binary function—that is, it is *not* true that either you are creative or you are not.

Binary creativity is no more true today than it was for our ancestors of 20,000 years ago. All people can to a certain extent be creative. And a lot of people are creative without knowing it; others think that they are highly creative and are not. But clearly it's possible to have more or less creativity.

Let's take some people who are exceptionally creative and ask; How would these people have behaved 20,000 years ago? Okay, they were *highly* creative. But what did they do on those days when there was nothing to be creative about, that is, no crisis, no problems? They found solutions for problems that didn't exist. They were always *doing* new things and being their usual assertive and aggressive selves. Occasionally they invented something. If you start rubbing wood together because you have nothing else to do, you may find that it's a good way to make a fire. But if you want water, it's not of much use to start rubbing wood. So if you are always indiscriminately doing new things, you don't know in advance what you will produce—fire or water. Usually that's not too profitable.

Dealing with Loss

Now to add further confusion, I'd like to discuss what appears to be a completely different subject. Imagine an old lady. She lives alone and has only one friend, her little dog. Of course, she pays a lot of attention to him. She feeds him, pets him, grooms him, and walks him through the town. And she talks to him all day long. She loves him very much. But one day the dog gets out and is killed by a truck. The old lady becomes completely distraught. She's lost her best friend. It's as though she herself were hit by the truck. She doesn't eat and can't think of anything else but her poor dead friend. One day she walks into town and suddenly finds herself standing in front of a pet store. And in the window of the store is a little dog. She goes in and asks, How much? The owner knows of her sad, recent loss and gives her the dog. She thanks him profusely and takes the little dog home, feeds him, tries a lot of names on him, and talks to him all the time. She's completely happy again!

Why is she happy again? Remember, her first dog is still as dead as it ever was. And she's always known that there are little dogs in pet stores. So nothing has changed. Yet she really is happy. How is this possible?

We think we know how this phenomenon works. If there is love or affection by one person for another person, or for an animal, or for an object such as a car (or a new product or research program), it is said that you give a part of yourself—of your own personality—to it. You lose a part of yourself and give it to, in this example, your little dog. And it is very important that this part of yourself be accepted.

So in a sense we can say that there is a transmission from you to the receiver. And along this transmitter/receiver line there's the potential for love, affection, or whatever you want to call it. What happens when the dog dies is that the part of her that's in the love object dies. Now what happens when she sees this other little dog in the pet store window? She starts taking away that part of herself from the first dog. She takes "herself" back from the other dog and gives it to the new one.

That's an important ability humans have. Otherwise, life would be impossible for us human beings, given that we have this tremendous brain. This ability makes it possible for her to establish a new bond of affection with this other dog.

Now there's a lot in this that relates to the death of anything, including a research project or an idea in a company. Every individual involved in a development in which he or she has put a part of the self now has a little black dog.

Any Road Won't Get You There

When a dedicated climber is surrounded by a number of mountains he wants to climb and has only a short vacation, he wants to start climbing any mountain immediately. Now the mountains are covered with clouds. So he really doesn't know where he's going, but he starts climbing anyway. But if the man who wants to climb the mountain sees an open sky—sees where all the mountains are—he can identify his goal and creatively strategize the route to take to get to the top. Climbing in the fog—without a clear focus—offers a small chance of success, for once he reaches what he thinks is the top of the mountain, it turns out to be only the top of an adjacent hill.

Creativity is wonderful, but when it has no focus, it can cause aggression, troubles, fights, internal competition, and irrelevant "inventions." On the other hand, the same creativity well focused is always the basis of, and critical to, the development of successful products and enterprises. Therefore, creativity is only a tool like a surgeon's scalpel or a writer's typewriter. You can use it either well or poorly and get results that have nothing to do with the scalpel or typewriter. Creativity is exactly the same. It is extraordinarily useful, and you can't miss if you use this instrument with knowledge and a goal.

Motivation—Internal or External

Eric Fromm, in his book *Escape from Freedom*, defines happiness as the feeling that results when a positive expectation is fulfilled. So that means when a person wants to feel happy, he or she must first expect something. And, secondly, it must be positive. And it would be even better if the individual could contribute to the fulfillment of this positive expectation program. When it is fulfilled in the manner the individual expected, a feeling that we describe as happiness results. So the formula is: A positive expectation program, fulfillment by our own efforts, and the feeling of happiness results.

Let's look at this more closely. Imagine a man in his big, new, expensive boat sailing in the sun on a calm sea. All of a sudden the weather changes and it becomes cloudy and stormy. He can't see anything. Suddenly there's too much wind, and in a terrible storm his boat is hurled on a rock, which puts a hole in the bottom and it starts sinking. He launches his dinghy and gets in. He realizes he's in a bad situation. But somewhere out there is a fellow watching his radar. He sees a big dot first, then a small dot. So he concludes what happened and calls the coast guard.

Now the local lighthouse keeper starts flashing a light in his direction. Our sailor sees the light and starts rowing towards it. Finally he sees that the distance is becoming smaller. "I'm going to make it!" But the lighthouse keeper also sees that the distance is closing and thoughtlessly turns off the light. Suddenly, our sailor is in a panic again. When he doesn't arrive on schedule, the keeper turns the light back on. Again the sailor starts rowing, feeling he's going to make it. Twenty yards . . . ten yards . . . one yard . . . he makes it and is *very* happy! His big, new, expensive boat sank, but he is very happy because he has fulfilled his life-saving, positive expectation program by his own efforts. When the light went out, he lost this program and was immediately unhappy again. What did the lighthouse keeper actually do?

If somebody has an expectation program, everything is okay. If you can motivate yourself even in exceedingly demanding crisis situations, we call that having a "survival mentality." You have the ability to supply yourself with positive expectation programs even in dreadful situations. But if an individual cannot self-generate such positive expectations, you can often give him one. That's what we call motivation. I can sometimes motivate myself. But when I'm not self-motivated, a friend, my wife, or my boss can sometimes give me such an expectation program.

Shared Focus Leads to Cooperation

Some time ago at AKZO, we invented a method to add different scents to plastics. When the public heard about it, they sent many suggestions. One was, "Can't you add a scent to garbage bags so that cats and dogs don't tear them open?" We thought this was a marvelous idea. We took a group of creative people from sales and R&D and put them together in a room. We gave them the task of figuring out how to realize this idea. In no time at all the walls were covered with big sheets of paper, and we had hundreds of ideas. One interesting idea that surfaced was to use the scent of lions or tigers. There was so much enthusiasm for it that some people went back to their labs and started mixing and blending things—because they believed in the idea.

We also searched a data bank of biological abstracts for recent literature on animal repellents. We got patents, articles on tests, and so on. In fifteen to twenty minutes, we walked out of the computer room with a file on all known repellents. Now we were able to take everything we had so far and go to market research and say, "Can you give us a feel for the size of the market for a product like this?" When we got that piece of information, we went to production and said, "If we have a market of about this size, and the formula of the product is this, can you produce it for a price level of around x?"

Then a group of six or eight people from the patents department, research, market research, lawyers, production, and so on got together and found multiple problems. Their solution demanded creativity. And that was exactly the same creativity mentioned earlier.

And they did develop the "perfect" product for keeping dogs and cats away from garbage bags. But while they were enthusiastically solving a host of small technical problems, thereby making use of all their creativity, an amazing statistic surfaced from their tests. Eighty-five percent of cats and dogs tested avoided contact with the scented product, and it worked perfectly. But the other 15 percent couldn't care less. No possible solution could be found for this phenomenon.

Management's Role

So we decided not to market the product and to stop the project. But the researchers didn't want to. It was then management's function to see to it that these creative and highly motivated people were not demotivated.

And to deal with that problem, management had to make use of both creativity and human sensitivity. Because left with the death of their small dog, we must prevent part of them dying, and eventually their creativity and motivation as well.

Now let's throw all these stories together and see what they tell us. First of all, creative people are more action oriented and aggressive than people in general. So they are often not easy to be around. Second, when creative people are surrounded by other creative people, they can behave like the lady and the dog. You can imagine what the consequences of this type of behavior are in an organization.

How can these examples help us better understand, motivate, and "manage" highly creative people? Take any organization that feels the need for innovation—it's not important whether it has 10 or 10,000 people. It strives to find and bring together people with demonstrated creative abilities. Then management says, "Ladies and gentlemen, we have an important need—creativity, so help us out."

They've already made at least two errors. First, they don't realize that demonstrated creativity in another organization is no proof that these individuals will be creative in *this* organization. Second, and more important, the organization is trying to let their creativity loose without a clear objective and focus. The most creative ones go into action immediately and bring along their assertive and aggressive characteristics. So you'll soon have a situation that is typically found in organizations dominated by highly creative people such as television studios and advertising agencies.

These people continuously generate the products of creativity. They're also continuously struggling for the continuing existence and development of *their* ideas. A lot of time and energy is lost in their individual struggles. And it's caused directly by the management that gave them the unspecified directive—"Be creative!"

Realities of Hypersensitivity

Onto another area. People working in functions or on projects in which they invest themselves, can be hypersensitive, judge themselves and others too harshly, and even get pugnacious. This has a lot to do with dealing with creative people in companies. And again, we go to the fundamentals.

I pop in on some neighbors—a husband and wife. The husband opens the door and I enter, look around, and say, "Where's your wife?" They've been fighting, and I can "smell" it. He confesses: "Okay, we had a fight over a T-bone steak. She cuts off too much of the fat because she doesn't like it; she *always* takes off too much." And while he's telling me this, he's getting madder and madder all the time.

So you start to think this guy is crazy. Can he really be *that* upset about the fat on the T-bone steak? That's impossible! And it is.

What he's actually doing is fighting with one of the computers in his brain—the one that weighs, evaluates, and balances everything out all the time. This particular computer tends to say things like, Have you done this?, You missed doing that, You failed here, or, You did that wrong. This computer's function is to put things back into balance again, so when it feels you've done something wrong, you have to be punished. And people punish themselves in a spectrum of ways from watching a television program they don't like to having a bad mood and being unpleasant to someone else.

We are so intelligent that we have all found some rather clever ways to punish ourselves. Now if a part of yourself is in your partner, he or she is a convenient first target. If you punish your partner, you punish yourself. That's the way it works. So this guy is not fighting about the fat on a T-bone steak or his partner's "sloppy" work; he's angry with himself for something else. So he's out of balance. And his partner is always in a perfect position to be the vehicle for self-punishment. Being aware of this phenomenon may help managers understand and better manage some of their creative-people problems.

The Value of Sponsorship

A talented physicist finds a method to predict the physical and chemical properties of certain alloys and writes a computer program that makes his ideas operational. The use of his system reveals promising new application areas for specific compositions, and these appear to be economically feasible. Of course, each potential application needs to be studied further with respect to technical development, market development, and so on.

Now the problem surfaces when our creative physicist starts adding up all the man years needed for the realization of his ideas and puts the total in his report. Multiplied by the average cost of a man year, it's an astronomical figure. So as many people had predicted, it was all too good to be true. But rather than abandon the work, let's add the element of "controlled creativity"—focus. Our physicist is advised to select the most promising area and work out a plan for it in detail, setting targets for technology, product, and market. The plan is presented again and accepted.

One side effect of this whole process is of great importance. Creative people in research departments observe that the moment the idea they are working on becomes an official target and gets support from other disciplines, it's as though the sky has cleared for climbing the mountain. At that very moment the chance for success becomes greater and greater all the time, along with the excitement! Now research people can present their work to those who really decide on budgets and funding. They *love* to have the support of management who can contribute to their goals. This is the opposite of NIH—the "not invented here" syndrome.

This is invented everywhere, at the same time, contributed to by different people. From our experience at AKZO and the experience of many others, this is the formula for success: Focus, commitment, management support, cooperation.

4

BUILDING THE GROWTH TEAM
How to Assign Roles and
Change Cultures

In the late 1960s and early 1970s, when we were just learning our trade, we typically found ourselves being hired for business growth programs by executives from marketing or R&D, or by the CEO. We were particularly thrilled when it was the head honcho, because we felt that dealing with the top person ensured a higher probability of implementation and a successful outcome.

However, what we learned painfully over many programs was that if marketing sponsored the effort, manufacturing or R&D inevitably became less than enthusiastic about moving forward with the results—in other words, the NIH (not invented here) attitude raised its ugly head.

This was equally true for sponsorship under any other auspices. To our naïve surprise, we found that even the CEO and his staff fared no better in trying to establish a growth opportunity they had conceived of implementing within the organization. This was even more dramatically displayed when the CEO had attempted to come up with a business opportunity for one of his divisions. So we learned that it was almost impossible for a corporate-sponsored growth program to ever find support from a division.

TOP MANAGEMENT SUPPORT IS CRITICAL

Some of the valuable lessons that came out of these frustrating experiences included the fact that to be successful, the search for new growth opportunities must be multifunctional. But most companies are organized functionally, and each unit is headed by an individual with clear goals and responsibilities— and sometimes hidden agendas. Therefore, in most companies, expecting a single function to make something new happen that will inevitably impinge on other functions is not realistic. And companies almost always have a "cultural" bias, that is, they are primarily led and oriented in the direction of technology, manufacturing, sales, and so forth. Yet, any new opportunity will require the participation and support of many or most functions to be successful.

The other critical lesson we learned was that any effort undertaken to identify and implement significant new opportunities must have the genuine, visceral support of top management—the movers and shakers, the decision makers. Without this, bright people can work hard and long somewhere in the bowels of the organization without ever producing the fire to accompany all the smoke.

Finally, the organization as embodied in the top management group must clearly recognize the need for a concerted effort to identify and implement new growth opportunities. And here we mean a real, emotional commitment to undertaking an effort that can, at the least, be uncomfortable. Many organizations give only lip service to the need for growth, so tangible results never occur.

THEY'D BETTER OWN THE GROWTH PROBLEM

Axiomatically, the members of the growth team must be those individuals who *own* the growth problem. If the objective is growth in new areas not already addressed by the company or its divisions, the growth team is best comprised of executives at the corporate level, because they typically would have a broader, overview outlook. And if the opportunity is to be implemented outside an existing division, involving divisional people in a completely unrelated area has little merit.

Also, divisional people typically are less than enthusiastic about spending time away from their core responsibilities, those from which their compensation and bonuses derive. When the search for new products, services, or other growth avenues is directed to the needs and benefit of a division or group, then the leadership in it must be involved. They are the most intimately knowledgeable about the unit's capabilities and goals, and the output will be of direct consequence to them.

WHO SHOULD BE ON THE TEAM?

One approach to making decisions about participation is to ask the following questions: Which individuals will be required (or involved) in implementing a successful outcome? Who could develop an NIH attitude if they were not involved in the process?

On most programs there is representation from the respective groups that will be responsible for manufacturing or delivering the product or service, marketing it, selling it, developing it, and financing it, as well as from the CEO or ultimate decision maker within the unit. Also, if a company has unique or special functions, those should be represented. For example, a toiletry company might have a high-level executive responsible for fragrances or colorants.

In some companies, fortunately, there exists a culture that is team oriented, and individuals tend to get together formally and perhaps even informally on a regular basis. This tends more often than not to be a positive factor in pursuing a growth opportunity. However, in a large number of cases the functions operate almost totally independently and seldom have any face-to-face contact among their responsible heads. This presents the challenge—or opportunity—of creating a cohesive, dedicated growth team.

Promoting Cohesiveness

Once the functional areas that will be represented are established, the next step, ideally, is to identify specific individuals who will be interested in and supportive of such an undertaking and, thereby, will personally nurture and help guide the process. However, our experience says that after the establishment of criteria everyone supports, those individuals who initially were less than enthusiastic eventually become part of a committed team because their thoughts and goals are represented in the criteria. Also, the bringing together of individuals for special situations intrinsically leads to a team-building effect. In designing a group, it is best that the members be peers in terms of responsibility and authority. If this is impossible, imbalances can be dealt with under the appropriate circumstances and with the right leadership.

This group will be establishing the guidelines and directions for doing something outside the traditional. Everyone involved must recognize that many people view creativity as a threat. But the rational process of focusing it at a target with which the collective problem owners are comfortable greatly reduces, if not eliminates, this source of potential problems.

The real task is to establish a united front at the responsible management level and attempt to eliminate the schizophrenia that often results when management talks about creativity and growth but lacks the emotional commitment to support rational growth actions. Such attitudes are easily sensed within the organization, and they can bring any attempts at growth to a dead stop.

PHASE 1: LOOK INSIDE FIRST

There are essentially two phases in the pursuit of a new growth opportunity:

1. The growth problem owners assemble, establish the criteria for success, and take the other steps that will ultimately produce specific actionable opportunities.
2. Designated personnel qualify and, ultimately, successfully commercialize the opportunities that have been created.

Functionally and organizationally, both steps require different teams for different purposes. The tasks of the first-phase team are as follows.

1. Establish a rational set of criteria that will predefine success. These should be heavily oriented toward exploiting the existing strengths of the organization, if relevant.
2. Identify and select opportunity areas that promise a high potential for meeting the criteria and that point the direction for the organization's growth.
3. Creatively identify or generate specific actionable ideas, "properties," and potential collaborations.

Our twenty-plus years of experience lead us to state emphatically that the key decision makers should be active participants in steps 1 and 2 of the first-phase team tasks. After criteria are established and approved and an opportunity area for growth has been selected (see Chapter 6), step 3 can be delegated.

The biggest problem we find in companies is that management seldom ever does, or even participates in, steps 1 and 2. Then, lacking any guidelines or direction at all, it delegates step 3—finding the specific "magic ideas," properties, and schemes for collaborations.

CONTINUITY OF THE SEARCH TEAM

We find that most participants in the first meeting, designed to have the group establish the criteria, want to stay on for the subsequent events and, usually, through the entire program, culminating in the specific identification of promising opportunities. Apparently, the highly participative, focused process is stimulating, educational, and fun.

However, some executives are intrinsically uncomfortable in the required ambience and are anxious to escape the process. Although not optimum, this is acceptable after the "pointing of the way" and can be accommodated after the establishment of criteria. Individuals who drop out early in the search quite often appoint their number two, whom they may view as emotionally and intellectually better suited to participate.

Another point about the composition of the team is that when the project begins, the opportunity that will be pursued and the specific actionable vehicles that will be used are still unknowns. Therefore, when the objectives come into focus during the process, individuals with more relevant expertise can be added to the group.

A word about size: Responsibility and involvement tend to decrease in direct proportion to the size of the group. Experience says that a maximum of ten individuals can feel intimately involved. They, in turn, can go back and report to and involve their own subngroups so that the events can be promulgated widely, if this seems appropriate. But having more than ten executive participants, all of whom are articulate and high powered, leads to a lack of individual commitment, poor group dynamics, and extremely long and tiring meetings because everyone must be adequately heard.

TEAM BUILDING

Building the growth team is no different than building any other team. A team spirit results when a group of individuals shares a unique, common experience. One example is Jimmy Doolittle's Raiders, who shared the experience of a carrier-based attack on Tokyo. Some forty years later these individuals still meet once or twice annually to reminisce. Another example is what happened when the lights went out in New York City during the famed East Coast blackout of 1965. Individuals who normally would not have shared the time of day with each other found themselves suddenly stuck on an elevator or in a subway. Thus thrown together, these people shared a unique, harrowing experience that also led to fast friendships and annual reunions.

Participation in this "search for the future" is something that most people consider important to the organization and potentially their careers. So there intrinsically is an element of team building in such activities. Anything that can be done early on to give the project visibility and importance also can be helpful. For example, the person with the most visibility and prestige in the organization, perhaps the corporate chairman, could host a special dinner to bring the participants together and launch the project. Such an effort could emphasize the group members' singular status and highlight their important roles in this critical undertaking. Also, getting the group away to a new, exciting environment sometime during the process—especially if it includes one or more nights spent together over drinks and dinner—can be another positive contribution to team building.

The benefits of having a team rather than a group of individuals becomes apparent when they manifest their support for each other in the more creative phases where infant ideas are potentially put at risk. A benefit of achieving visibility and prestige for the group is that the right individuals may become interested and want to become involved when the implementation phase is being designed and staffed.

CHANGING THE CULTURE

The following is a generalized description of a typical business meeting. Regardless of the number of participants, between two and three individuals dominate the event and do all the talking. The others lose interest, become frustrated, and tune out. The number of ideas discussed is usually limited to one or two. No visible record keeping takes place in spite of a lot of talking. Closure, if there is any, is overly intuitive and tends to be dominated by the last subject or idea discussed. Politics can easily surface. Criticism and judgment are the dominant modes.

When the subject matter is the future of the organization—and creativity will play a role in finding and establishing this future—all the characteristics just mentioned are decided negatives that need to be changed or eliminated. One critical cultural change is to allocate equal time to the participants regardless of rank. Interestingly, we find that the top-ranking individual is often pleased to be "another banana in the bunch" and not feel responsible for controlling and moving the group. A simple way of achieving equal airtime is to make it clear that every issue requiring an opinion will be polled individually around the table. Most often, those who normally talk too much are happy to be relieved of the responsibility and actually find themselves listening to, and being impressed by, what others have to say. The theme that we like to promote is embodied in the phrase "All of us are smarter than one of us." And it's true.

THE EXECUTIVES CREATIVITY WARM-UP

When INNOTECH professionals have the responsibility for managing a group of high-powered executives in a working session, the program team brings the participants together the evening before and runs what has come to be known as an executives' creativity warm-up. The rationale is that business executives are selected, trained, and encouraged to be analytical and judgmental. This is the mode in which they spend most of their time and where they make their major contributions. However, when subjects are going to be discussed that do not have three decimal places associated with them, and where new ideas will be entertained and tentatively developed, these thinking styles are inimical to the required ambience.

The key points that must be hammered into the heads of a group of executives, if they are not going to get in each other's way, are few, but critical. The first goes back to Alex Osborn's early work with brainstorming (which we discuss further in Chapter 9). It is a principle that states: "Quality is a function of quantity." Given this premise, it's important that a number of ideas be proposed, discussed, and built on. Yet we've asked groups of executives, "When you have a meeting in your organization for the purpose of addressing a problem and coming up with some solutions, how many ideas are typically discussed?"

When asking that question in the United States, Europe, or Japan, we've gotten the same responses 98 percent of the time. The number is usually two, with a few groups stating three, and others only one. Having so few ideas to consider practically guarantees that they will be the most obvious solutions and devoid of any creativity. And the reason that so few ideas are discussed comes down to the typical meeting style, which intrinsically includes bad group dynamics. An idea is proposed, and immediately several individuals begin to find fault with it. Sometimes the remaining meeting time is exclusively devoted to this far-from-creative function. When two ideas surface, the task then becomes to compare them.

Underlining this lack of idea productivity is the core problem: failure to understand that individuals or groups cannot simultaneously create and evaluate ideas. Rules should be established so that specific times can be set for doing one or the other. But the group members must clearly recognize that pursuing their normal meeting style of doing both simultaneously is *totally* counterproductive.

At this point the role of the acknowledged top man or woman is critical. If the leader cannot control himself or herself and thus allows the habitual luxury of knee-jerk judgments, everyone else will follow this lead and the meeting will be unproductive. Instead, efforts to find "What's good about it?"

in an idea or proposal change the dynamics of a meeting dramatically and lead to constructive building. We've often seen an idea filled with flaws be converted into something of great merit as a consequence of this exercise and the willing participation of a group.

And this tendency to judge does not follow the stereotypical assumptions of most people with regard to functional areas. We have seen financial and engineering executives play the creative game with gusto and be consciously aware of the need to defer judgment. On the other hand, we've seen totally negative, noncreative CEOs and professionals involved in supposedly creative functions. In one case, on a program conducted for a company in The Netherlands, the chairman and the managing director (equivalent to our president) were so disruptive with their negative, schoolboy-like behavior that we were forced to terminate the meeting abruptly and take them outside the room. We then pointed out that their behavior was destroying an event they were paying for both in dollars and the time of their people. We also noted that if they refused to change, there would be no alternative but to cancel their attempt to identify growth opportunities. Having gotten this message across, they were able to recognize how critical their appropriate behavior and performance could be to the entire undertaking. This example also shows that the individual in charge of a meeting must have enough confidence and authority to go after some high-level troublemakers.

THE BENEFITS OF GETTING IT ON PAPER

In most business meetings lots of talking goes on, but little, if anything, is written publicly that is visible to the participants. Consequently, there's seldom any hard copy record or feedback from a meeting, and employees within the culture start to believe that most meetings are a total waste of time.

A simple mechanism to attack this problem is to have flip charts or other mechanisms available that will allow the participants to see their comments, ideas, and insights collectively unfold. An individual can be assigned this responsibility, or it can rotate among participants. The task of the "scribe" is to record the information exchanges as succinctly as possible.

One subtle point that seems to have some bearing on the electricity and dynamics of the event is that the scribe should try to write down exactly the words that were spoken by the contributors, rather than editing. An individual is usually not overly pleased when an editor poorly translates his or her words. It feels much better to see your thoughts written as expressed and to read what you had to say.

Often a meeting should result in closure—a consensus decision on action to be taken. However, if nothing is written down during the course of a one- or two-hour meeting, attempts to achieve closure prove difficult because participants cannot remember many of the comments and contributions. However, if they're written down and in full view of the group, they can be referred to—used as mnemonics—and can play a valuable role among other mechanisms that may help a group reach a consensus complete with actions to be taken. Another benefit is that these sheets can be cleaned up a bit, typed, and distributed as feedback to the contributing participants.

THE TEAM THAT WILL "RUN WITH IT"

Some time ago, a well-meaning paper company ran an advertising campaign with the message that there was no stopping an idea. They talked about the power of an idea, and the accompanying illustration showed a brick wall with an ordinary yellow wood pencil driven through it.

Nothing could be further from the truth. We believe they did our business world a disservice by promulgating the theme that an idea was so powerful it was unstoppable. The reality is that new ideas are no stronger than infants. They both need a great deal of support just to survive, let alone to grow and develop fully. That takes a dedicated and committed implementation team.

So once a management group has worked through a rational process, identified an area of promising growth potential, and supported it with specific vehicles for moving ahead, the next—and critical—phase of the effort begins.

One of the benefits of having the growth problem owners involved in figuring out what to do is that when the usable ideas are ready for implementation, the individuals who participated in the process can be valuable sponsors and supporters. In this role, these people can run interference for the champion or champions who are spending their days trying to bring the new ideas to successful commercialization. The champion desperately needs this sponsorship.

Try to Staff Inside

How do you get a collection of individuals to work as a team? When you can staff the growth team from people already in the corporation, you have a jump on success. When you have to search outside for the skills necessary, you increase the risk of failure. Doing something new is enough of a challenge without having to "learn" a new company and figure out its culture. This is especially true if the assignments are viewed as temporary, or worse yet, part-time. Each participant must feel that he or she really is a team member whose future depends on the team's performance.

The Champion

As we have pointed out in previous chapters, the individual who will be given the responsibility for successfully commercializing something should volunteer for the role. Or, when this individual is approached, he or she should very much want to be a part of this exciting challenge. The task of the executive responsible for identifying and establishing champions is to try to find the right fit between the opportunity and the individual. This right fit will go a long way toward ensuring a committed, enthusiastic champion rather than a reluctant appointee.

Sometimes it is feasible to identify one or more individuals who will eventually have responsibility for commercializing the output. Some of the benefits of early selection are that the individual can actually be a member of the growth team and, therefore, be intimately involved in the creation of the specific opportunity. Also, a member of the growth team has a terrific opportunity to build a rapport with key executives who can make his or her job easier later on, when he or she has to call for support from specific functional areas.

There are, however, benefits to the selection of the champion *after* the creation of the ideas. A primary benefit is the greater likelihood of getting an individual with the right knowledge and experience matched specifically to the known opportunity.

Champions who are enthusiastic about their role tend to develop the charisma required for their leadership of others. They tend to attract others to the cause and to spread their enthusiasm and commitment throughout the fledgling organization. If the champion does not have enthusiasm and commitment for the opportunity, another champion must be identified.

In this role everyone must clearly understand the high risk potential. Many people conservatively state that three out of four new opportunities pursued will fail. Others go somewhere between an overly optimistic 50 percent to an experience-based 90 percent. In any event, successfully commercializing a new opportunity is a high-risk venture, and management must accept this and allow for failure.

Finally, to change the culture in a supportive way at this phase sometimes means establishing new supporting mechanisms. These will allow the necessary development and commercialization steps to be taken more simply and quickly than would be possible elsewhere in the organization's bureaucracy. A dedicated champion and his or her team will work diligently to fight bureaucracy. Although the normal bureaucratic mechanisms may be required and may serve as positive factors in the operation of more mature businesses, managers must smooth the way for the champion's many unique needs—one of which is fast turnaround.

ANOTHER VIEW FROM THE REAL WORLD

Robert J. Schaffhauser

Dr. Robert J. Schaffhauser has had a distinguished career in business management, R&D, and "doing new things." He was first exposed to INNO-TECH's process as executive vice-president of Signode Corporation. Bob played a key role in a Planned Growth *program when he was the sponsor of the company's highly successful new ventures program.*

After Signode's buyout by ITW, he served as executive vice-president of the parent company before joining Chemical Waste Management as vice-president for business development.

Congratulations, dear reader: you have identified a promising new venture and have decided to proceed. You are about to embark on perhaps the most exciting, frustrating, exhilarating, depressing, career-making, career-busting experience of a lifetime!

I would like to describe a few of the pitfalls that lie ahead and suggest some defenses.

The Credibility Problem

The first subject I'd like to discuss involves the projections and aspirations the members have for their venture and how these might affect their credibility.

Because entrepreneurial managers tend to be optimists, they often project an overly aggressive scenario. Then Murphy's law *always* intervenes (in manufacturing, technology, sales, legislation, etc.), and a credibility gap is created.

New things—products, services, collaborations, and so on—almost always take more money and happen more slowly than originally anticipated. Because they're new, you're usually breaking new ground in manufacturing, technology, markets, and company familiarity. And when you're involved in new frontiers, there are more surprises—usually negative surprises, bad news, unexpected hurdles—than one experiences with established businesses. Nobody, especially executives who are used to running established core businesses, likes bad surprises; in fact, they *hate* them. When one gets involved in new things, very strange things happen. And when very strange things happen, the news is not always accepted as a necessary cost of pioneering. Rather, difficulties are often looked upon, even subconsciously, as negative reflections on the management competence of the venture group. So what often happens is that after a few years when all the lumps have been taken, all the disappointments have been overcome, all the problems have been solved, and *finally* the business is really ready to take off, the team is replaced with a new one. "Now that this is beginning to generate substantial revenue, let's put some businessmen in charge." Let us not mistake this last thought with the fact that the skills necessary to manage a large business are different from those required in a smaller one or that some entrepreneurs would prefer to "step off" when a business ceases to be a startup and "go do it again."

There are a few things we can do to mitigate against credibility loss. First, we have to make sure that top management is better prepared to understand the rules of the game. They should be prepared to accept technology shifts, delays, and so forth not as mismanagement or a venture going sour, but as a likely event in the unfolding of a new frontier. But also, venture teams have to be more careful not to make promises that they cannot deliver. I don't believe this is an actual "between a rock and a hard place" dilemma where if you project realistically, you'll never get the project approved. I think one *can* project realistically and win proposal approval.

The one thing I see missing from most plans is the presentation of adequate upside and downside scenarios. If a venture team takes the time to show how things *might* go wrong, and if they show what they plan to do about it, bad news does not come as a terrible surprise, and no one loses credibility. Management has been made more confident that things aren't simply out of control. That's the key. This approach makes it a little bit easier. Confidence is not completely lost, because you have anticipated possible problems and have *credible contingency plans to deal with them.* I don't believe that entrepreneurial types overproject deliberately. Perhaps in their enthusiasm they truly believe that this business is going to do that well, and they lose sight of the fact that it might not. We're not suggesting that they should lose their vision, but that they should project a detailed downside scenario and not simply give it lip service.

You Can Use Your Best People

In putting together a growth team—especially in a small, new, untested situation—there is the temptation to assign the people that happen to be available. Unfortunately, the people who are available may not be up to this type of assignment. In considering the *best* people in the organization, management sometimes feels that it cannot move people out of critical positions in the core businesses. They are sometimes tempted to take a few people who are between assignments but have never had operating responsibility and put them on the new venture. It really doesn't make any sense. What's the solution? What we did was to deliberately reach into the core business and take a few of our "stars"—those, of course, who seemed to have new business building talent and interest. Then we incentivized them so that the venture was worth pursuing. And we immediately supported each one's number-two person to take over all core business responsibilities. We were very pleasantly surprised. In the main, the number-two people did a very good job. They were far better prepared to take over than some had thought. Now it's true that when significant decisions had to be made or difficulties arose, the experienced executives weren't totally out of the picture; they got called in. But almost all of their time went into making the new venture succeed. I suggest that it is possible to take some of your better people out of their jobs, assign them to new ventures, and win on both fronts.

Management Commitment Is a Must

Many times the new business is not looked upon as essential or mainstream but merely incremental—or "gravy." We're conditioned to structure and plan our core businesses so that when they grow and do what they're supposed to do, the company will be fine. We then look at these new ventures as "icing on the cake." When you view new business as merely icing on the cake, it doesn't really get the commitment. It doesn't get sufficient management attention. And it clearly doesn't get all those other things that a new venture deserves—and needs. But if you were to view these growth opportunities as essential to the corporation, then you would treat them differently.

You may have a situation where the chairman says, "Everything is fine, but I have a few extra dollars, so I'm going to invest something in new business development. See what you can do, and come back to me in a year and let me know what happened." If so, I can absolutely predict that you might as well save your money. He has zero emotional commitment. He doesn't even want it in the plan: "Don't include it in our future earnings projections because I'm not sure this thing is going to materialize. I don't want to mention it to the board at this time."

On the other hand, if the future of the company is thought to depend on new business development (and it often is!), it should be included in the long-range plans as an objective that must be met: "I'm going to discuss it with my board of directors and commit to certain objectives. And I'll want to review the progress of this fragile, but important, new venture frequently." Think of the difference within the organization as to how this opportunity will be pursued.

I strongly believe it's more of the latter that we must emphasize in many U.S. companies. Too often in U.S. industry new things are looked upon as opportunistic forays. If they work, great; if not, no great loss. I don't think you can approach new business development this way. Unless top management is seriously committed, incentives alone won't make people perform, because it's their understanding of what top management expects that really motivates. If the leader doesn't put himself on the line, nothing is going to happen. It becomes an intellectual exercise.

The Insider Sponsor

When it comes to funding, cooperation with the rest of the organization, and internal power and politics, the growth team needs a sponsor who is part of senior management. He's the one committed to helping them survive and succeed. He represents them in court. Preferably the sponsor should be an old hand in the company—a senior executive who's been there a long time. He knows the company's culture and has the confidence of the board and the rest of the management team. When you bring in a sponsor from the outside—and sometimes that might be all that you can do—no matter how good the guy is, you've compromised because he doesn't have the other necessary qualification or ties. He really should be a "good ol' boy." If he is, he'll do a lot better than any high-performance, fast-track, hotshot. The champion, too, should be an "insider," but an outsider *might* work here. But for the sponsor, forget it. In my case, a number of companies have come to me and said, "We've read all the articles you've written and heard that you've started up and run some businesses very successfully. So how about coming here and doing it for us?" My initial response usually is, "Don't you have some talented senior guy in-house that could do it?"

Don't Rely on the Core Business

Often in starting a new business you count on tremendous contributions from your existing core business. You count on extensive sales, manufacturing, and R&D support. This also is true when you make an acquisition. You find a little company that doesn't have sales, for example, and you say, "When I bring you into my company with our 500 salespeople, your sales are going to boom!" In reality, you've got to be very careful not to expect too much from your core business. If you expect your salespeople to drop everything and suddenly start promoting this new product, you're mistaken. Or if you expect sales management to permit it, you're also mistaken. If you expect the engineering department to go out of its way—to put aside some high priority things in the core business—you're really mistaken. And if you expect manufacturing to go out of its way to support the trials and tribulations of this new product, you're incredibly mistaken.

Some new business plans I've seen talk a lot about synergy and make very eloquent statements along those lines. But the plans are too heavily dependent on immediate, active cooperation from the core businesses; and most probably, you're not going to get it. You'll get some, but you'll have to put together your team and way of doing business so that you're not overly dependent on core businesses. They have other fish to fry and a budget to meet. They have to meet sales goals of $3 or $4 billion, and you're asking them to sell $2 million of your new thing. Your little business disappears in the rounding! And you certainly can't expect senior management to bang the table to get a major piece of their time. Yet every new venture expects it to happen. "Gee! They've got 500 salesmen out there; look at all the help we will get." It just isn't going to happen.

One reason it isn't going to happen is that salespeople are reluctant to present things that are strange to them. They're uncomfortable talking about them when they don't have the answers. And sometimes new things cause an awful lot of work. They present the new thing, and they're immediately hit with five questions they can't answer. They've got to go back and get the answers—and understand them. Then they've got to go back and present these answers—a lot more work for a few sales dollars!

Fortunately there are steps that can be taken to encourage sales support. A salesman in a mature business has been calling on the same customers for years and is running out of things to say. And he knows he's got to continue to call on that customer just to know what's going on—hold his hand, make an appearance, and all those good things. But meeting after meeting is getting more boring. He's got nothing new to say. He really doesn't. Don't expect miracles, but giving a salesman the means to make his calls more interesting will bring rewards.

There is another approach that may help. We did the obvious; that is, we trained them, gave them literature, and so on. But then we'd say, "Look, we're not asking you to make any dedicated sales calls for this new business, but we would like you to mention it." We don't expect the salesperson to spend a great deal of time or get involved in any detail. All we ask is that the salesperson find out if there is any possibility that this customer could possibly use this product or service. If there is, the salesperson has a preaddressed postcard, and all he or she has to do is write down the customer's name, phone number, and a one-sentence description of the opportunity and drop it in the mail. Of course, it goes to the new business team, and they screen it by phone. If it turns out to be a good lead, we'll personally call on the prospect and invite the salesperson to come along if interested. If we close the sale, he or she receives a commission.

We found this postcard system to be relatively painless and effective. And the other thing that makes it good is that at the end of the month if a salesperson hasn't submitted any postcards, it's glaring. So there is some pressure on him and he's likely to say, "Gee, I'd better send in a couple of these things." And at just one card per salesperson, with 500 salespeople, it sure is going to keep the venture team busy. But believe me, without the cards you'd be lucky to get five leads from 500 salespeople.

Reading from the Same Script

When it comes to new ventures, every key executive from the very top management of the company on down has to be reading from the same script. I've run across situations where a venture is very familiar to the division president because the business growth team discusses their plans with and reports to him. Then sometimes a year downstream, you suddenly find out that the chairman hasn't been kept sufficiently informed by that division president. So he starts asking questions concerning the new business: "What are we doing that for?" "Why don't we do it this way?" [which is a drastic change in direction]. So it's imperative for that division president to get to the very top of the company *early* so that once the venture starts getting hot, you don't find you have to change direction.

Sometimes—but, fortunately, not terribly often—you get a superficial buy-in to start the project. But you really haven't described to the very top management of the company in detail what you're going to do, how you're going to do it, and where you're headed. So a year later, when it's time to accelerate the implementation, you find that you have a civil war at the top about how this thing ought to be handled—and that's a disaster. It's imperative that communications at every level be superior right from the start, and the sooner the better. Get everybody involved and get their commitment. Get them involved as much as you can, and keep them informed so that there's no excuse later for coming in with a radically different change of direction.

5

ESTABLISHING THE RIGHT CRITERIA
How to Balance Vision and Realism

After over twenty years of working with companies to help them try to generate new growth opportunities, we have concluded that the two most critical elements in the success of any such undertaking are *focus* and *commitment.* Establishing the right criteria is a giant step toward realizing both of these. Getting together the growth problem owners and spending the time required to hammer out a good, solid set of criteria probably constitute the highest return-on-investment event in which a group of executives could participate, because this event and its resulting criteria will be the cornerstone for the success of any and all growth efforts.

On the other hand, companies that don't have such a set of guiding criteria, and the focus that emerges from them, can easily flounder into irrelevance and ultimately disappear in spite of all their frenzied activities and the dollars and time wasted in shotgun searches for magic ideas.

CRITERIA ARE A UNIQUE "FINGERPRINT"

When INNOTECH was formed in the late 1960s, we had a nagging fear that we would soon work ourselves out of business. We thought that after we'd run a growth program for a chemical, consumer product, or steel company, we would be precluded (due to conflict of interest) from working in these industries again, at least for many years. But when we started to generate criteria, we found that although companies served the same market, the criteria they generated to guide their growth efforts were so unique that they led to completely different opportunity areas and, ultimately, results.

After many years, we have never seen one set of criteria even remotely resemble another. Thus, a set of criteria are a company's unique "fingerprint" derived from the management group, which is heavily biased by current needs, strengths, capabilities, and goals.

There are no right criteria for a new growth undertaking any more than there are right criteria for the perfect husband or wife. Everyone has his or her own concept of an ideal mate, otherwise, we would all want to marry the same person. And many pointless arguments can be avoided if one recalls the Latin phrase that translates into "In matters of taste let there be no dispute."

OF COURSE WE (DON'T) HAVE CRITERIA!

Probably 50 percent of the companies we ask, "Do you have criteria?" avow that they do. Yet we hardly ever see any that are specific enough, tight enough, and complete enough to serve their needs fully.

Most companies rely on the kind of criteria that investment bankers are accustomed to using: about half a dozen criteria that are mostly financial. These serve the deal makers well because they are not searching for tactical opportunities as much as screening specific companies.

Criteria for proactive business growth must provide far more that a screen against which opportunities are evaluated. They must be directional and, in essence, embody the company's well-conceived strategy. So we invariably find that what people are calling criteria—and then wondering why they are not useful—are merely screens. Furthermore, some executive groups say they have criteria but then confess that those are not written down—because "everybody knows what they are." This statement is about as accurate as that of the blind man holding the elephant's tail who declares it to be like a snake.

Everyone thinks his or her own idea of criteria should be fine for everyone else. Nothing could be further from the truth. Executives who have been working together closely for twenty years are often greatly surprised by what their peers espouse in a meeting designed to flush out and collectively generate a set of workable criteria.

Our finding is that each individual can usually suggest about a half dozen, and these, more often than not, are dominated by financial ones. This occurs because most executives do have specific financial standards they use almost daily to measure the performance of their core business and make decisions on investments. But the more intangible factors relating to the pursuit of strategic directions are often incomplete or almost nonexistent.

WHAT DO CRITERIA DO?

Criteria build a team and begin to generate a commitment from that team. In addition, they serve as a screening mechanism allowing decisions to be made on the basis of something other than intuition or politics.

Criteria also serve as a mnemonic system that constantly reminds all the growth problem owners of their original goals. As the saying goes, "When you're up to your ass in alligators, it's easy to lose sight of the fact that you're trying to drain a swamp." And new business development certainly has its share of alligators lurking about.

Finally, certain criteria can be creatively useful in that they establish a direction and, in so doing, enhance creative productivity in a particular area or force a particularly creative way of thinking.

One example might be a criterion specifying that whatever the new opportunity will be, it must strengthen a particular functional area such as marketing or technology. Having something like this on the list tends to get people to become creative about how they can integrate this goal into opportunities under development or consideration.

Different Kinds of Criteria

Criteria developed for different purposes and within different organizations tend to have slightly different constructs. A set of criteria guiding the efforts of a group to find new applications and markets for a material will be heavily oriented toward specifying and characterizing the material. The business and marketing side will be light, because the objective is to identify not a new product but additional sales opportunities for an existing one.

Criteria generated at the corporate level tend to be a little more general than those developed at the division level, and they are typically heavy on the financials. Here, as few as a dozen criteria may suffice. But a set generated for a division will typically number eighteen to twenty-three, because they tend to be far more specific about capabilities.

Criteria Are *Not* a "Wish List"

Simply stated, the difference between criteria and a "wish list" is reality. Anything can find its way onto a wish list. But criteria take a vision and temper it with the hard facts of life. A key component of reality is to establish the level of risk that can be tolerated by this particular group of growth problem owners. In essence, reality becomes heavily influenced by the probability of success.

Pressure plays a vital role in establishing criteria. Does this particular management team have only one shot in a highly intense, time-critical situation to achieve growth, or do they have the luxury of some time and more "bullets"? If this is their only shot, the criteria will be heavily influenced toward much lower risk and a shorter time frame.

Bill Parker, an INNOTECH vice-president, calls this situation the "second serve phenomenon." In tennis it makes strategic sense to power serve the first ball over the net, making the return more difficult *if* it lands fairly. This strategy is supported by the fact that one still has a second serve. If needed, the second serve is far more carefully controlled and accurately placed at the sacrifice of go-for-broke power. In some ways, management groups tend to act like tennis players.

Criteria Represent a Growth Strategy

Criteria establish hurdles, highlight strengths, and imply next steps. They may even target markets. Collectively they represent a growth strategy. Therefore, if a group of executives establish a set of criteria that prove unachievable, these criteria and the strategy embodied within them must be revised and, typically, be opened up to allow more options to be generated.

Given the particular need of an organization and the personalities of its management, some criteria will be unnecessarily tightly focused and close to home, leaving no flexibility to explore new avenues. Meeting such criteria poses many problems, which are sometimes insurmountable. Others seem to promise a high probability of success.

GOOD CRITERIA SHOULD BE . . .

First, good criteria should be as tight as realistically possible. Having suffered through many years of "Can't you just give us something we can make money with?" we've learned conclusively that the success of any new business growth effort is directly proportionate to the specificity of the criteria and resulting focus.

The ubiquitous Sunhook line of plant-hanging hardware offers us some excellent examples of how specific criteria can be. Among the program's twenty criteria were the following:

- *Must:* Product's critical components not to exceed two and a half square inches of plan area, or thirty-five grams of zinc
- *Desirable:* Product line with a retail price not to exceed five dollars

This list highlights the fact that the only good idea is one that fits a company's capabilities. A good set of criteria should enable a manager to screen out quickly 90 percent of ideas that surface from any source. That clearly can save enormous amounts of time and money.

Keep in mind that the weighting of a criterion as a must or a desirable is a mechanism for adjusting its importance within the group. As a rule of thumb, it is better to craft a criterion into a must, because musts tend to delineate limits. For example, it is better to have a must minimum sales goal of $50 million rather than a desirable of $100 million. Desirables do not clearly delineate "walk aways," and a list of criteria dominated by them tends to be too loose.

The final test is that the normally eighteen to twenty-three specific criteria must be internally consistent with each other. We have often heard the question, What happens if you can't achieve the resolution of a particular point? We pondered this for many years before finding the answer. A complete set of criteria that are internally consistent are like the pieces in a jigsaw puzzle. Invariably, after almost all the pieces are in place, the size and shape of the final one is no longer determined by opinion. Logic takes over, and the only answer that will resolve a particular issue within the framework of a given set of criteria is X. And because logic produced that conclusion, there are seldom any losers.

BENEFITS OF GOOD CRITERIA

One of the many benefits of a well-wrought set of criteria is that they flush out amorphous and intangible "feelings" into a set of tangibles. Thus, the target and mission become clear. And with this clarity comes the elimination of an enormous amount of wasted effort, time, and money.

It's a bit like the sculptor who was asked how he managed to create such a remarkably lifelike statue of an elephant. His reply was, "I just took away everything that didn't look like an elephant." Being able to eliminate opportunities that don't look like the one you are seeking leads to all kinds of benefits. Management looks a lot smarter, and folks in the trenches trying to identify these opportunities get a morale boost.

In coming up with success criteria, a group must address many critical issues that have been left unresolved for whatever reasons. Because the criteria have been created by the group of individuals who own the problem, they are the product of this collective entity and not the personal, often self-serving, creation of an individual with his or her own agenda. Therefore, participation in their creation gives each individual some degree of ownership and comfort in the resulting output and offers both the individual and the group a feeling of significant accomplishment. They have now pulled their thinking and goals into a collective rational focus they can all believe in and support.

Finally, woven throughout the many specific points are the signposts that show the way to a domain in which to begin the search for relevant growth opportunities. And this domain has come into focus precisely because it fits what the problem owners want to do; leverages their capabilities, strengths, and resources; and fits their culture.

HOW FAR FROM HOME TO LOOK

One strategy that makes enormous sense is to search for growth opportunities as close to home as possible in order to utilize the maximum number of strengths and resources the organization possesses. Searching in this domain reduces the risks inherent in moving further afield, and, consequently, results in much greater comfort.

So, given that criteria are not a dreamy-eyed wish list, one critical issue that must be addressed is, How far are the members of this problem-owning group willing to stray from their tried and proven path?

A related question that needs to be addressed is, Should the new growth opportunity be sought via internal growth or externally via acquisition or another form of collaboration? We've been in situations where a company judged its internal development capability to be so weak that the program focus was strongly biased toward external avenues. We've also been in situations that were just the opposite. So there are truly no rights or wrongs or opportunities that are perfect for every company.

If an organization desperately needs growth and feels it does not have the time or resources to pursue development on its own, the strategy of choice quickly becomes acquisition. In the majority of programs INNOTECH runs, all the options tend to be left open until the specific actionable items surface. Then the decision is made vis-à-vis the specific opportunities to pursue commercialization via either acquisition, internal development, joint venture, license, or another creative form of collaboration.

GENERATING CRITERIA

Well-intentioned, highly motivated management groups tend to ask the question, What should we do to prepare for this event? To their surprise, the answer is Nothing. Furthermore, they are actually encouraged *not* to prepare, because we have found that independent preparation tends to bring individuals into the event with fixed positions, rather than letting the collective group entity wrestle with, and resolve, the many issues that must be addressed. So the first creative act in an excursion to generate new opportunities is the creation of the guidelines.

If at all possible, leadership of the event should be sought from the outside. Although it is not impossible to run a successful criteria-generation event with an inside leader, the probability of a successful outcome is jeopardized because of a number of factors that are difficult, if not impossible, to eliminate.

One of the greatest things an outsider brings to such an event is his or her "license to be stupid." An insider cannot ask "dumb questions," which often turn out to be not so dumb at all. An outsider has a far greater chance of being totally apolitical. Also, an outsider is not blinded by "the obvious" and, therefore, can challenge it. Often, what is assumed to be a given turns out to be no longer relevant or vital.

In any event, the individuals attempting to facilitate the event must have superior listening skills, because often the real content emerging from the group will be found between the lines rather than on them. Many criteria are never stated aloud but are ferreted out by implication. And the degree of emphasis individuals give to a particular point may be a significant factor in the establishment or wording of a particular criterion.

One point that should be emphasized to the participants is that there are no right or wrong answers. There are just answers, opinions, and information that in total provide the raw material from which the requisite criteria can be drafted. Not surprisingly, some people of lesser rank would be intimidated in such a critical event that deals with the future focus of the organization.

The objective, then, is to strive to get essentially equal participation from all the players by polling them in a round-robin fashion on the various issues under consideration. And the assurance that there are no rights or wrongs can be helpful in allaying some concerns.

Many times participants report that this was the first time that the usual few heavy talkers did not dominate. This pleases them, and they feel that they have been heard at long last and have contributed personally to the ultimate result—a long step in generating collective commitment and support for the eventual output.

TEAM-BUILDING BENEFITS

By working together and sharing this unique experience, along with participating in the individual events that go into a successful new business development program, a group of strong-minded individuals evolves into a team that functions far more smoothly—one where there are more gestures and comments that support friendship. Also, if all the participants focus on the same goals—embodied in the criteria—they will cooperate in achieving those.

Recognizing that all executives are equal, but some are more equal than others, each participating executive realizes that he or she will lose some authority in a team setting. Those individuals who cannot tolerate this thought or see the benefits in it are not often found in such a meeting. If they do accidentally wander in, however, they are a major source of disruption.

As most managers in high-level positions have found out, they may be the engineer on the train, with hands on the throttle controlling all the horsepower; but any conductor can pull the emergency brake and bring the entire train to a screeching halt. Interestingly, in business it is especially easy to pull this brake by doing nothing. Knowing this, wise managers have long recognized the value of enlisting their teams in support of a rational common effort.

So managers clearly have good reasons to trade off their management prerogatives. The management group's commitment to and support of an objective reached by consensus produce benefits throughout the organization.

HOW BIG? . . . HOW SOON?

Two questions are crucial to the total integrated structure of a set of criteria: How big? How soon? The answers to these two questions shape and guide all the other criteria. The How big? issue is important because we are trying to recognize reality. Flights of fancy must not push the size criterion beyond what an organization can realistically finance and handle.

Setting the minimum size that makes sense is also significant. We find that this issue of size is most often addressed by dollar volume of sales. There are other situations where this criterion tends to be set as an absolute number of profit dollars contributed to the organization. If the undertaking is too small, it quickly loses the attention and support of the participants. Therefore, size must not only justify the effort but also fit realistically within the expectations that can be supported by investments and personnel.

Of equal importance is the issue of timing: When will we benefit from this effort? Knowing whether the focus is short or long is important in the development of the supporting strategies and criteria.

RANKING STRENGTHS

An exercise that groups genuinely enjoy is the delineation and ranking of their strengths. This is talking about good news. A simple rule to establish is that there be no debate about any named strength, because the last step of the exercise, after all the strengths are listed, is to identify the top third. In so doing, the ones that receive little or no support in the polling process quietly float downstream. Enormous time and energy (not to mention ego blows) are saved by this approach.

Traditional thinking says that after we categorize our strengths, we should then list our weaknesses. Do so at your own peril! Discussing weaknesses is a distincly negative experience for the group. No one enjoys it, ugly politics can surface, problems become exacerbated, and nothing of benefit is gained.

A simple change in the task can produce a better result without the trauma. It now becomes not What are our weaknesses? but What new strengths would we like to see? This simple re-

framing eliminates the many negatives, and people can participate far more positively and creatively.

MEETING ENHANCERS

Although we discuss meeting dynamics at length in Chapter 7,
we want to offer some specific ideas here. Our counsel is to
write down everything collectively on flip charts or similar
devices and also individually on paper. We have found that four-
by-six-inch cards are a convenient format for the individual participants, and the cards can easily be collected, shuffled, and
sorted.

When you give a task to the group, allow them two or three
minutes to write their responses on a card. This produces a
breadth of coverage, because one gets the collective thoughts of
all the participants. In contrast, a question as normally posed to
a group produces an individual with an answer, whose presentation of that answer gets the other participants away from the
question. The results are a narrow band of responses and the
potential for debilitating, time-wasting controversy.

Giving each individual time to think and establishing that
each will be called on in turn greatly increase the output. Also,
this way of running the event intrinsically gives the facilitator
far more control of the dynamics and the participation. This is
obviously a plus when the group members are high-powered,
far-from-bashful executives accustomed to getting their own
way and dominating discussions. In Chapter 7 we discuss various aspects of group dynamics in more detail.

PHANTOM CRITERIA

After many years of working with executive groups to generate
criteria, we discovered what we now call "phantoms." Phantom
criteria are real, but for a variety of reasons they have never

been verbalized. These are the statements and judgments that kill a project when they surface, often very late and after much time and investment.

Any company operating with less than around twenty specific criteria sooner or later will be plagued by these phantoms jumping out of the bushes. No matter how well run a criteria-generation event is, there will invariably be two to five phantoms waiting to be flushed out. A simple approach for doing this is for the leader to propose—in series—up to a half dozen "test ideas."

Whether these ideas have any merit is not terribly relevant; the leader uses them to flush out from the subconscious minds of the participants issues that have yet to surface. The procedure is this: The leader presents an idea to the group and gives each individual an impossibly short time to make a go/no-go decision. (We use five seconds!) In that brief period individuals will, after fighting with the facilitator over the illogic of the proposal, come up with a yes or no.

Now the task is for each person to figure out why he or she said yea or nay. This process will surface reasons, comments, and insights that have not been expressed before during the event. Typically, from this exercise, the group will also become more aware of some of their deeper cultural motives.

RATING CRITERIA

The last step in fine-tuning a list of criteria is to have the group discuss and establish a rating for each criterion. These do not have to be precise. Such simple categories as the following will do.

- *Musts:* We like to define musts as establishing "walk aways." This means that if a particular opportunity does not promise to deliver a must criterion, the group will "walk away" from it.

- *Desirables:* Desirables are the criteria that the group will work hard to accomplish. If all the musts are met, the project will proceed.
- *Bonuses:* Finally, the bonuses are nice, but not worth any extra effort. Interestingly, however, bonuses often turn out to be quite useful creatively, and they frequently become upgraded to desirables or musts. If this occurs, it suggests that the group felt certain criteria weren't very important at first but changed that assessment after moving through a rational process.

WHAT'S GOOD ABOUT SUCCESS?

Given that the pursuit of the new opportunity will be fraught with dangers, discomforts, pain, and all manner of unpleasant things, a good exercise to run at the conclusion of a criteria-setting event is to have the participants verbalize the benefits they feel would result from successfully meeting the criteria. This typically produces a list of about twelve to fifteen points that show the group's emotional support for the undertaking.

These mutually recognized benefits can be of great assistance in helping a group weather the storms. It also is of benefit to run the same exercise from a personal viewpoint and ask what benefits would accrue to each one individually. In this case, there's no public profession, but merely the realization that there could well be some personal advantages coming out of this undertaking. The most common one that CEOs share with us is "I get to keep my job!"

ONCE CRITERIA EXIST . . .

A good set of criteria become broadly valuable and get used quite often to assess various opportunities. Once adopted, they become part of the culture, especially if they are promulgated broadly. There is no harm in communicating them downward, and it's critical that they are taken "upstairs," especially if a higher power in the organization or at corporate headquarters should have been involved in their creation but was not.

Exposing criteria to the ultimate decision maker will preclude unpleasant surprises later on. Typically, a meeting to discuss them will generate some minor fine tunings which contribute to the sponsorship and buy-in of the leader. Once they exist, they have the amazing ability to infiltrate the subconscious minds of not only the growth team but many other individuals in the organization, and they start focusing search efforts into more productive arenas.

CRITERIA CAN CHANGE

Criteria are not cast in stone. In fact, criteria should be reviewed every few months to see if any of them need to be changed. This can mean deleting some, adding new ones, or changing their weighting. Typically, however, a list of criteria will last the duration of the search. We're aware of some that have been used effectively for several years.

If criteria are changed, they tend to be changed in certain directions. But from our experience on several hundred programs, less than 50 percent are changed *at all* during the six- to ten-month search effort. This is in spite of the fact that the group is actually encouraged to revise them whenever necessary. Only less than 10 percent of changes are substantive, and of these, less than half ever really affect the strategic direction of the growth effort.

Typical changes are upgrades or downgrades. A criterion addressing the subject of proprietary status tends to be upgraded as the program nears the implementation phase. The size of the undertaking tends to be reduced as reality is confronted in the investigation of various opportunities. Time to commercial introduction tends to decrease as sales or other business pressures mount during the hunt. And increasingly today, acquisition becomes the implementation strategy preferred over the other options that were under consideration at the onset of the program.

Finally, we've heard many times that "You can't get blood from a stone." Likewise, you can't get a good, tight set of criteria from certain groups that have not really wrestled with many of the necessary realities. Therefore, some undertakings begin with criteria that are admittedly too soft and, therefore, not very useful. However, as the work effort proceeds, there are many opportunities for learning and revisiting. Consequently, these criteria tend to firm up early enough to be useful in the ultimate evaluation of opportunities that emerge.

ANOTHER VIEW FROM THE REAL WORLD

L. Richard Chasen

L. Richard Chasen has been intimately involved with creativity and new products since the early 1960s. He has held responsibilities in advertising, new business development, and in line management as general manager of Homecraft's Hardware Division—a subsidiary of U.K.-based Coats & Clark of Glasgow, Scotland.

Dick was head of new product development for Homecraft and championed the creative growth program that led to the highly successful commercialization of the well-known Sunhook line of plant-hanging hardware. Dick currently has marketing and new business development responsibilities for hardware and houseware for the Homecraft Consumer Products Group, a subsidiary of Coats Viyella of Glasgow, Scotland.

Criteria give some discipline to your business. In creative sessions you let the ideas go where they want to, and then, in a separate session, you are "critical" of what was created—you match it up with the criteria. And those that fit, you develop further.

Maybe the creative output would be better earlier if the criteria were a little bit tighter. Ideally, you would like to have them as tight as possible. But sometimes it takes an educational process within the growth team before they are willing to get that tight. We know that the tighter the criteria are, the greater the probability of success—because everybody knows the kind of thing that's going to come out. It won't be a big surprise.

Sometimes they just can't make them tight enough at the beginning. It's not that they don't want to; it's just that they don't have enough perspective yet. But that usually comes a little later.

Right Criteria Have to Come from the Heart

Sometimes participants are not sincere; they are *playing* the game without *feeling* the game. In fact, one of the criteria should be: How really serious are you about this new business growth program? Are they doing this for political reasons, as an exercise or an ego trip, or because the president wants it?

If these are the reasons, you'll never see anything commercialized. We've been involved in a number of programs, but only one was very successful. I can't say the others weren't successful. It's just that they weren't pursued. And one of the major reasons they weren't pursued was that we had the wrong criteria. They weren't "sincere" criteria. They came from the mouth, not from the heart. They were "window dressing" criteria.

Stay Close to Home

If you go to a trade show like the Houseware or Hardware Show, you can walk down an aisle and say, this is a vacuum-forming house, this is an injection molder, this is a screw machine house. You know immediately what their core business is because they want to keep their machines running. That's what we did. We stretched, and we bent, and we went crazy to make our new product a die casting. It was a very strong criterion.

On the Sunhook line we didn't have any distribution in plant care. Yet, because we were lucky enough to have the encouragement of our president, we went plunging ahead with it.

Why? We all felt good and got excited about it. He really was a man of vision. It never would have happened if we had had a common, short-range-thinking manager. Today the game is, What can we "wrinkle" with current technology and bring to commercialization within the next year?"

Every Function Should Be Represented

In our program we made sure we had criteria from the key people representing all our disciplines—financial, manufacturing, sales, marketing, and corporate. The corporate criteria were our growth aims. We covered margins, what the up-front investment could be in tooling, and what kind of inventory we could handle. We said we would put in that assembly line and do this and that. We'd even set up a factory and so forth. And we got our interest in using our die casting machines in there because we have 147 of them on the floor.

The nature of our business is cyclical, and there's no control over it. So we were really going after something that would help us here. When I look back at it, maybe the criteria put too much emphasis on keeping those machines busy. But it seemed like a good idea at the time. And it worked!

Good Criteria Work Hard

From our experience I think it would be valuable to develop a system to evaluate the validity of criteria. Because criteria are like a business plan, you really should try to develop valid, truthful ones which you'll be able to bring to management and say, "Hey look, we need new proprietary products, and these are the kinds I want to look for."

For example, I can say in the criteria that it's highly desirable to get a mechanical patent. This would bring something new and exciting to our game. So part of developing criteria—one reason why you should do this— is to communicate clearly to top management what you're trying to do. And all of them really should be involved in it. The nature of our business is no longer just manufacturing or engineering. Today we're really a marketing company. But we need the financial people, the marketing people, and the salespeople in order to make something a success. That's why they all have to be represented in the criteria.

New product criteria are essentially a strategy for growth which can end up in a business plan. That's how important they are. Many times you have a strategy and business plan, but you really don't have any criteria. That's like a "wish list," because you're not specific about how you're going to get there. But once you have a set of criteria, then you know where to look and how to go about it.

Plan equals structure, and structure equals discipline. Structure, discipline, and process are all key words here. There's a point where you must freeze your plan. If you're designing a product, there's a time when you finally have to say, "We're going to make tools *now!*" That's discipline.

Criteria let you measure. You can then say that a product concept stinks or it's good—it fits or it doesn't. You can match them up. When you get to the phase where you have to evaluate concepts, you can get all the right people together and say, "Hey, these are the concepts that came up in our creative session; now we're going to evaluate them using criteria." If you don't have criteria, you can't decide.

They Can Keep You out of Trouble

Criteria are a basic religion with me, because here's what can happen when you don't have any. Say you're a houseware manufacturer, and you have strong distribution capabilities. You also have excellent product design capabilities. So you come up with a product that's an incredible idea in *electronics*. It's not your business. You said you were going to come up with salad spinners and other products in your area. And all the thinking and approvals have gone into an area that has a perimeter. Now someone comes up with an electric cake decorator. It does everything! So, all of a sudden you're into small electric motors. You're into a totally new system. You might as well be going into a totally new business—because you would be. But you have criteria. And criteria will keep you from getting sucked into an area where you don't belong.

Otherwise you'll rationalize it: "I can sell it." "Good return on investment." "Good this." "Good that." You're almost certainly going in doomed to failure. Criteria say focus and discipline. That's what's behind new product successes. Once a group comes up with a focus, they generate a commitment to that focus. And without *commitment*, you're not going to get anywhere; and without *focus*, you're not going to get anywhere. In new business development, discipline gives you enthusiasm for the *right* thing.

They've Got to be Realistic

As I look back at the failures we had, some of them were because the wrong criteria were set. Not enough time was spent on formulating criteria. However, our scope when we went into the plant-hanging hardware was contained within reasonable criteria.

As soon as we tasted success, the world was our oyster. We could do anything! So we said, "Wouldn't it be nice if what we were selling cost fifteen dollars per item instead of a buck or two? Look at the margins and all that good stuff."

Our logic was right, but our organization was wrong. So we found this terrific product. I was full of enthusiasm. Everything was good except that it couldn't fit our manufacturing criterion that we should make the thing ourselves. We couldn't engineer it, we *really* couldn't engineer it. Our engineering knows die casting. And all of a sudden we're into motors and bearings and all kinds of stuff. We're way beyond what we are able to do. We just bit off more than we could chew because our criteria were not realistic. The criteria were not truthful, and they were very fuzzy because we were afraid to make them tight. We were afraid of tightness.

The Leader's Commitment (or Lack Thereof)

We didn't have the backing of the guy in charge of it. He didn't believe in it enough, so he really didn't support it. I remember another situation where we were focused on wiring accessories, and we had a number of ideas for fittings based on a clam shell concept. They were injection molded and had strain relief bushings and all kinds of features relating to wiring accessories. It was the right time; it was within our technology; it was within our distribution.

But we didn't go after it because, again, we didn't have the support of the key guy. And the reason we didn't have his support was because he wasn't involved in generating the criteria, so he hadn't bought in. It's fundamental that the key people be involved if you're really serious about moving forward and commercializing *anything*.

6

GENERATING AND EVALUATING NOVEL IDEAS
How to Find and Assess Opportunity Areas

When INNOTECH was formed in 1969, we viewed its mission as generating novel ideas—the concept of an opportunity area had not yet surfaced. We brought together teams of people and, in essence, brainstormed. From today's perspectives we entertained a lot of people. But little ever happened of commercial worth until we discovered what today we refer to as a "cornerstone insight."

That insight was that *there is no such thing as a good idea.* This means that an idea in itself is neither good nor bad; it's just an idea. What makes an idea good or bad is its success or failure. And in business, a good idea is one that makes money.

SUPPORT FROM THE PROBLEM OWNERS

Armed with new insights, we started to try and figure out why ideas succeeded or failed. Our first answer proved to be a half truth. We concluded that *companies* make ideas succeed or fail. In reality, we ultimately found that it is not the entire company that is involved with the development or commercialization of a new opportunity. Rather, in every instance, no matter what the size of the company, there's a group of people who "own the problem."

These problem owners are what make any idea for a technology, a market opportunity, or any growth vehicle succeed or fail. So we ultimately learned that the problem owners would give an idea the support, attention, and commitment it needed to be a success only when they understood and believed in it. If they didn't, the idea—regardless of its merits—was destined to fail.

Our experience in the United States, Europe and Japan leads us to believe that at least 85 percent of the time, effort, and money that companies put into looking for new opportunities is totally wasted. We say wasted because these resources are spent on projects and in areas that will never gain the support of the decision-making, problem-owning group. This is because the projects often do not maximize the company's existing resources and do not have the market potential to make a meaningful impact on the organization's future.

These insights led us to work closely with the problem owners of our client companies in order to develop a tight and realistic set of success criteria that would characterize the "right" new opportunity, thereby greatly improving the probability of its ultimate commercial success.

DO YOU REALLY WANT A NOVEL IDEA?

In the late 1960s and early 1970s, our emphasis was almost totally on novel ideas rather than rational growth strategies. It took years before we began to view an idea simply as a vehicle for helping a company grow and be successful.

Then we realized that many companies also viewed novelty as a liability rather than an asset. They felt, often rightly, that truly new ideas required pioneering, greater amounts of money, and greater risk—more "pain" than existing ideas that had already gone through this painful birthing process at the financial and emotional expense of others.

Many executives also saw that the first company to introduce a novel idea made visible mistakes which they could then avoid, often allowing them ultimately to take over the market. That is why today an important part of generating criteria for a Planned Growth program is to establish clearly whether the growth problem owners really have what it takes to pioneer a new-to-the-world idea successfully.

So the first question to ask when getting involved with ideas as potential growth vehicles is, Do we really *want* a novel idea, or would a new-to-us idea that fits well enough to have a high probability of commercial success make more sense? It should come as no surprise that since the 1970s fewer and fewer companies have had the patience or long-term view to pursue truly new opportunities.

Risk aversion runs strong. But rather than leaving this subject on a negative note, we hasten to point out that high-risk pioneering has historically been the province of the entrepreneur and is increasingly so today. Established companies in their search for new opportunities spend much of their time and resources seeking out small companies or startups that fit their strategic goals. When they find one, the entrepreneur is often rather generously rewarded.

This reward system appears to be working well for both parties, the entrepreneur and the company looking for growth opportunities. And beyond the entrepreneur or startup we see small to midsize companies filling the same role for the large company, presenting its acquiring parent with a significant head start on an opportunity.

CRITERIA AND OPPORTUNITY AREAS

Criteria that clearly predefine success are critical (see Chapter 5). Their generation by the problem owners elicits commitment and, ultimately, the group's sponsorship of the opportunities that emerge to fit these criteria. They ensure efforts to use a company's existing capabilities and resources maximally, and they eliminate an enormous amount of financial and human waste by clearly describing what can be termed the "domain" in which to hunt for the opportunity.

The criteria eliminate most of the world's opportunities (because they wouldn't "fit" the company) and delineate the domain. This is the arena in which to search for the subsets called opportunity areas. Also, the domain suggests the type of expertise we need to bring together and stimulate in order to identify leading-edge trends and technologies, as well as to produce insights and obtain information into "properties"— companies' technologies, ideas, and so on.

As Lewis Carroll said in *Alice in Wonderland*, "If you don't know where you're going, any road will take you there." And if you haven't generated criteria sufficient to describe a domain, how would you know the areas in which to search for trends and changes that could lead to meaningful opportunities that fit? Also, the question, Which experts would you bring together for my session? can only be answered when we know the focus and objective of the session. All this derives from the domain, which in turn yields the specific opportunity areas that produce the actionable ideas to meet our realistic business criteria for success.

However, while a good set of criteria are of inestimable value for focusing a search effort, they are primarily evaluative. Therefore, they must be reformated into something looser—a format that will not only preclude premature judgmental thinking but actually enhance the creative search. These are the subsets of the domain—opportunity areas.

THE OPPORTUNITY AREA

An opportunity area is *not* a single idea; ideas are the end products of creatively searching an opportunity area. An opportunity area encompasses many related ideas.

Perhaps an example would best illustrate this concept. Several years ago, an opportunity area presented to one of our clients in the natural materials and chemical businesses was "infrastructure chemicals." The rationale behind this as an opportunity area (a decade or so ago) was that the infrastructure was sorely in need of repair (more true today). This would create opportunities for new products to address existing and emerging needs. A *specific* idea would have been a spray to revitalize a concrete surface. But that specific single idea would have been the end of the exercise. The merits of such a product would have been debated and tested, and the company would have moved forward or not depending on its findings. The difference is that an opportunity area can yield *many dozens*, at least, of related ideas.

FOCUS HELPS MORALE

When criteria have been translated into a domain and ultimately into opportunity areas, we can focus effectively on the search for a new growth vehicle, thus eliminating the waste of the undisciplined look-at-everything approach. One important benefit is that the greater efficiency provided by the focus inevitably improves the morale of the people involved in the search—as well as the organization at large—and increases confidence.

Direction for the R&D Staff

Our business culture apparently clings to the myth that those working in R&D should be left completely alone and that this unfettered freedom will maximize the probability of their coming up with another Xerox or nylon. After sufficient investment in this approach, management becomes frustrated and disappointed, saying, "We're not getting our money's worth out of our investment in R&D."

In the late sixties and early seventies, we worked with a major textile company and were friendly with the newly hired vice-president of R&D. As the R&D unit was a new function, he had been hired to build, staff, equip, and create a first-class facility and team. As the entity approached becoming operational, our friend approached the top operating management and looked for some guidance on where to focus the group's efforts. The answer was, "That's what we hired you for." Subsequent efforts to obtain *any* direction met with failure. So work began on a number of projects viewed by the R&D head as relevant. After enormous amounts of money were spent over a three-year period, top management felt that nothing of "significance" emerged. (Also, the industry had taken a severe downturn.) Both sides became equally frustrated, and the entire organization was disbanded and the facility sold. The entire cycle was less than five years. Ironically, a leading European company in a related field, with more "patient" money, bought the facility.

Having frequently been involved in R&D organization, we have found that researchers, like other human beings, like to be heroes and appreciate the opportunity to try. This happens when the managers can clearly say, "This is what we want to do, and if you help us to do it, you'll be accomplishing something in the best interest of the company." In other words, "You'll be a hero."

Therefore, from our experience, *specificity of focus* tends to work as a *motivator*—not the demotivator management seems to think it is. On the other hand, there's no harm—and possibly some benefits—in giving researchers limited budgets of unallocated time with which to pursue special interests. However, unless these special interests fit within, or are complementary to, the opportunity area, they may result in intellectual exercises—efforts that never lead to commercial benefit.

How a Lack of Focus Creates a Pandora's Box

An opportunity area provides the focus for formal or informal discussions in which the rank and file of the company, and not just research and marketing personnel, can participate and contribute ideas. What would happen if we opened the Pandora's box of organizational creativity *without a focus?* To characterize such an incendiary situation, consider what happened when one company decided to run an employee idea-generation contest. We counseled against it, but the planners had already set some gears in motion and felt obligated to move forward. As forewarned, they received close to a *thousand* submissions. The executive responsible for the program spent an enormous amount of time reviewing this can of worms and found that *none* of them held any promise.

However, he faced the task of selecting "winners" and running an awards banquet to present checks to people who had submitted inappropriate or useless ideas that would never be explored or commercialized. Plus, as we predicted, he had to offer explanations to all those who submitted ideas that were not selected. And for every person who sought an explanation, there were twenty or thirty disappointed—and, in some cases, angry—people who didn't bother.

In brief, the creative output of the entire organization dropped. Only considerable time, effort, and energy will return the company to even its former level of innovation. And these problems occurred with ideas submitted by employees, who should have known the company fairly well.

In another case, one involving the general public, a Tupperware executive once told us that his staff received about 10,000 ideas annually from their customers and dealers, and that it took two years' worth—20,000 ideas—just to get one they would move into development.

HOW TO FIND OPPORTUNITY AREAS

Change produces opportunities. If the world didn't change, every organization could go on addressing the needs it currently addresses. However, changes happen and they create both problems and opportunities—problems for the organization that is unprepared for a changing market or technology, and opportunities for the organization that is causing the change or exploiting it.

The biggest change producers are the macro trends that flow from social, political, technical, economic, and cultural developments, all of which tend to be interrelated. For example, when OPEC raised the price of oil, this produced, in some areas, a miniboom in furnaces for heating homes with wood. An increase in the number of homes burning wood created or exacerbated air pollution problems. Social attitudes against pollution in defense of the environment led to legislation to restrict or ban burning wood. This, in turn, produced technology to burn wood more cleanly . . . ad infinitum.

So to find growth opportunities, we must find changes that are producing situations that our strengths and capabilities allow us to address. Another reason to look for trends is that the pace of change opens and closes opportunity windows with increasing speed. If we address an opportunity that exists today and our time to commercialization is too long, the opportunity will have evaporated before we are ready to address and profit from it. That's why decisions regarding lead times and time to commercialization for a new undertaking are critical—often dominated by the industry or core market the organization serves.

Electronics, for example, is an extremely fast paced field. The time from development to obsolescence is certainly not measured in decades. Other more slow moving and changing industries afford a company the luxury of longer development and commercialization times. But given the rapid pace of change throughout our modern culture, it seems that every industry ultimately will be swept into, and affected by, the explosion of new developments.

Using Outside Expert Sessions

To find promising opportunity areas, we have found one tool to be most efficient and effective, from both a time and cost viewpoint: the outside expert session. In such a session participants from outside the company identify the trends and information that can ultimately be formulated into opportunity areas. Because a responsible management group will not commit to an area without sufficient backup information, it's inevitable that any area must be well supported. (See Chapter 8 for a detailed discussion of the use of experts.)*

Traveling around to interview and meet with numerous people is not very efficient, and although data bases are increasingly important in providing information for decision making, the information in them is not usually that current. We have found, instead, that carefully selecting and organizing a group of experts in an area makes us much smarter much faster. And if a larger number of executives from the sponsoring company have to satisfy themselves, they want to be involved. Thus, through an expert session we can identify an opportunity area more quickly and easily.

Turning "White Noise" into Meaningful Information

The organization of output from an expert session produces opportunity areas. Even a well-run session, by itself, merely produces "white noise"—bits and pieces of information, insights, and opinions. Turning all this raw material into useful opportunity areas requires hard work and research to generate the required supporting information and organization. Finally, when all the information is collected and supported, it must be organized to fit the criteria.

Again, with an opportunity area we can identify changes that are creating new needs, which, in turn, may lead to products or services that fit the organization's criteria. In addition to literature searches and electronic data base reviews, managers can benefit from interviews with appropriate prospects, consultants,

---

*Expert sessions can be staffed with outside or inside experts, or both. We almost always use outside experts for objectivity and the new knowledge they bring. An expert-to-expert session brings together inside experts who have questions about an area with outside experts who should have at least most of the answers. This type of session is used almost exclusively as an input to important decisions.

suppliers, and anyone else who might bring insights and objectivity to the ultimate decision to form or pursue an opportunity area.

In framing an area, we have found that a good test is to consider the following question: Does this area provoke ideas that have the potential to fit the criteria? Another quick and easy test is to describe the area to an associate and ask him or her to generate a few ideas about it. If the ideas are *not* what you expected, you have good reason to reexamine the way the area has been framed and communicated. In addition, this distinction shows why a single idea is not an opportunity area. The single idea only generates discussion around itself and its merits rather than being a trigger for the generation of other ideas.

The Importance of Having Multiple Opportunity Areas

If presented with a single opportunity area, top management must either accept or reject it. If an area is approved because no comparisons or choices were available, the result is seldom the confidence needed to keep a group moving toward the goal—successful commercialization—in spite of the inevitable obstacles and disappointments.

On the other hand, if *several* opportunity areas are presented (we have found the optimum number to be around six or eight), the comparisons are often valuable and enlightening. An area can then be selected on the basis of its merits and its fit with the preestablished criteria created by the selecting management group. Having a range of choices tends to produce a higher level of comfort, which, in turn, supports the commitment required for successful development and commercialization.

Serendipity

Our emphasis, of course, is on using a systematic rational search to identify novel ideas. However, this philosophy must be tempered by the realization that serendipity does sometimes happen, but certainly not on a timetable. Therefore, when an idea does surface that has merit, it should be pursued. There's a story that circulates in Sweden about an army manual on map reading. Supposedly, it states, "If the terrain and the map do not agree, follow the terrain." This also seems to be good advice when a promising idea serendipitously emerges.

CREATIVE PROBLEM SOLVING

Let's change our orientation for a moment and stress *personal* creativity. How should we approach problems when seeking a creative solution? We like to define the following steps;

1. *Problem recognition*—finding or sensing an unstable situation or disturbance
2. *Naïve incubation/gestation*—personal immersion, a time of reflection and quiet contemplation allowing subconscious manipulation, restructuring, and new pattern making
3. *Information/knowledge search and detailed preparation*—learning everything about the problem via factual information and expert opinion from diverse viewpoints
4. *Knowledgeable incubation/gestation*—personal consideration of unusual approaches and ideas, now melding naïve notions of step 2 with factual information and expert opinion of step 3
5. *Alternative-solution formulation*—group generation of numerous possibilities, using creativity-enhancing techniques
6. *Alternative-solution evaluation*—group rigorously tests possibilities using tough-minded methodologies
7. *Chosen-solution implementation*—putting ideas into action
8. *Feedback and reassessment*—judging by results and improving the original idea

A problem-solving procedure can be transformed into a creative one only by breaking constraints, especially subtle ones.

For example, it is often a mistake to get too smart too quickly. The conventional expert opinion, if applied too early in the process, can foul up the creative engine. You are led, however unwittingly, into preformed channels of thinking, boxed in by traditions, and strait-jacketed by so-called authorities.

Conventional wisdom is creative death. The easiest way to escape is not to get caught. If the task lends itself to it, develop your own ideas initially *without* external information. Your naïveté will be more ally than enemy on the creativity battlefield, more asset than liability on the innovation balance sheet. Then, only after formulating your own ideas, can you confidently confront the experts.

That is why we recommend putting a gestation or incubation step both before *and* after the information-gathering step, whereas normal problem-solving procedures put it only after. You must think through the problem by yourself before you consult others. Go ahead and brood; uncertainty, ambiguity, and doubt are all friends of the creative process. Experience tension, frustration, and stress. Making an exhilarating free-fall is not what creativity is all about.

EVALUATING NOVEL IDEAS

Fortunately, the evaluation of novel ideas is occurring earlier and earlier in development processes. Business history is replete with horror stories of how millions were lost when a company commercialized a novel idea without asking the marketplace if it even wanted it.

There was a time when companies believed so strongly in laissez-faire R&D that projects continued until the researchers or developers ran out of interest or things to do. Then, somebody would try to sell the product.

This is seldom the case today, but incredibly it still happens. In the 1970s, 30 to 50 percent of the Planned Growth programs we ran fit into the category of application programs.

Typically, the task was to identify markets and specific uses for a novel idea or a unique material, technology, or process. In some of these cases, the projects had been under way for up to ten years, sales had been minuscule or nonexistent, and management was finally asking whether this wonderful idea would ever come to fruition and return a profit. Almost always, the answer turned out to be no. Realistically, work should have stopped many years beforehand.

Today, the same percentage of our Planned Growth programs still fit into the application category. However, the significant difference is that the tough questions are being asked much earlier. Also, rather than gnashing their teeth about terminating a long and expensive development project, executives now express delight at getting a definitive early answer on true commercial potential, because an early curtailment can save the cost of many years of futile development. In fact, some companies' managers are so sophisticated in their market orientation that they'll attempt to research a potential development *before* any significant work or funding even begins.

Recently, we saw this happen at Union Carbide. A few top scientists had come upon an idea for a technology that theoretically would offer some marvelous physical properties. However, there were trade-offs involved, and a clear picture was needed of where the superior properties might find real-world applications.

Several expert sessions were held, supplemented by extensive market contacts and data base searches. The conclusion was that the technology would realistically offer minimal benefits, and the market size clearly could not justify development under the current circumstances. So the good news was that the project was shelved indefinitely, at considerable savings in money and energies. Furthermore, no one regarded this as a bitter pill, but rather as a realistic assessment that led to a rational business judgment. In the "bad old days," the technology would have been unquestioningly pursued for many years before anyone even bothered to ask the first questions.

You Need Good Information

For most companies, one disastrous or disappointing experience is enough. Everyone knows that significant investment decisions require adequate information and that greater risks or investments require especially good information. However, one can never expect the same depth or quality of information on something new that would be available regarding an area in an existing business. So managers who expect precision and detail may find it difficult to accept the type of information they get on new ideas or products. Given intrinsic organizational tendencies toward inertia, this perceived lack of information can serve as a convenient and safe excuse for not moving forward with *anything* new. Evaluating a novel idea simply involves lots of creative hard work. There's no magic involved and, to get at the essence, we can simply say it is a process of "getting smarter."

Even with all the hard work, decisions must inevitably be made on the basis of incomplete information. If one already has all the answers and there are no unknowns, the decision makes itself and becomes a nondecision. In a perfect world, the goal of evaluating a novel idea is to get all the answers and thus clearly recognize what to do. But given all the variables and unknowns inherent in doing something new, this perfect situation almost never occurs.

YOU CAN'T MEASURE WITHOUT A YARDSTICK

Because "a problem well stated is a problem half solved," the task of evaluating novel ideas is at least half completed when the ideas result from a focused search process. Evaluation implies that something is judged against some standards or goals. Criteria provide the objective, rational standards against which novel ideas and opportunities can be evaluated. On the other hand, ideas resulting from an unstructured, shotgun search are essentially unmeasurable against anything more specific than the usual parameters, namely, potential sales, size, growth, and profitability. None of these really address the most important question: Does this idea or opportunity really fit our unique strengths, capabilities, and goals?

Surprisingly, criteria also serve as a sales tool. Once a novel idea has been thoroughly and creatively evaluated using clear and specific criteria, the decision to support the idea can be defended with more than intuition or opinion.

We remember a case in which, at the critical juncture of a new product program, every executive on the new business development team was ready to move forward toward commercialization—except one. The other team members used the criteria—point by point—to convince that individual. They asked whether the new program would meet each criterion, and point by point he had to answer yes or probably. The drill worked, and the product line—plant-hanging hardware—was taken to market and resulted in tens of millions of dollars in profitable sales for Homecraft, a subsidiary of Coats and Clark.

Intuition—The Ultimate Decision-Making Tool

Although hard work, analysis, creativity, and research are essential in evaluating a novel idea, one must not forget the value of intuition in making a final decision. While intuition seems nebulous or "soft" to most business executives, much recent research has established its validity.

Knowing that the numbers behind a proposal or business plan are normally best guesses anyway, we counsel executives to use the numbers as a learning tool and a part of their evaluation. But the ultimate decision should have a large component of intuition—"gut feel"—in it. When an individual is making a decision based on the operation of the conscious mind, the only thing he or she can bring to that decision-making process is what can be remembered.

The subconscious mind, however, remembers everything the conscious mind has forgotten. So intuition may well be far more valid than all the analytical processes that have been brought to bear in evaluating a particular novel idea. Interestingly, studies have shown that executives who achieve consistently high profits rate high on tests measuring ESP, or extrasensory perception. Intuition may be even more important than we now realize.

Creative Evaluation Creates Success

We've seen literally hundreds of ideas with potential killed by uncreative evaluators and market researchers who simply asked consumers, "Do you want this?" When the answer was no, they didn't even wait for any comments that could have told them how to improve the idea. Such comments or suggestions often steer a project into a new and promising direction.

Consider a situation in which an idea for a square is taken out into the marketplace. The first series of interviews knocks off one of its corners. The second knocks off another corner. This process continues until we find ourselves with a circle. And this circle is exactly what the market wants and is willing to pay for. However, if the developers had not asked the right questions at the beginning, they would never have gotten to the circle.

One such situation emerged following a creative program we conducted for a Finnish company, Instrumentarium OY. The seminal concept taken into development was a portable, low-cost system to detect microhemorrhages. After years of tortuous creative work, what emerged was an ultra-low-field magnetic resonance imaging system with the principal market appeal of low cost. It was a long, arduous effort that would never have paid off without creativity.

Another example of the metamorphosis of an initial concept is a high-speed inspection system for bottles in breweries that was successfully commercialized by Thomassen & Drijver-Verblifa NV, a Dutch subsidiary of Continental Can. That product led to a similar system to inspect chopped tobacco and another to spot off-color, burnt, or out-of-spec plastic pellets.

These systems and others are now housed within a new company called Qualiplus.

Seam-Pilot, a laser vision system to control robot welders, ventured far from its starting concept because the robot's software was not "smart enough" to communicate with its "eyes." Consequently, the development team at Oldelft, a Dutch-based company, had to take a year-plus intermission to develop software that could do a job better than the one originally conceived. When your approach to the marketplace is open and creative, these are the types of developments that frequently occur.

ANOTHER VIEW FROM THE REAL WORLD

Russell Gould

Russell Gould was production manager, director of research, and, ultimately, vice-president of High Performance Plastics for Signode Corporation of Chicago. Signode is well known as the leader in strapping materials and systems primarily for shipping large volumes of product. Russ became the head of a pioneering venture team which had the mission of getting the company into a nonpackaging business that could provide the basis for future growth. Criteria focused on exploiting the company's uniqueness in high-strength materials. The opportunity area selected was "netting and webbing." From this emerged a number of promising new products. Three that were commercialized were geogrids for soil stabilization, a breakthrough in snow fencing, and "safe" horse fencing. Russ's experiences in developing and commercializing these, in addition to his many years of related experience, are the basis for the insights and examples he shares with us here. Russ is presently president of RG Associates, a consulting firm to the plastics industry.

You Don't Need *Ideas*—You Need *Usable* Ones

What do we mean by ideas? There are two different types. There are "out of the blue" ideas. But the second and more important kind—the ones that I think are meaningful—are the usable, commercial ones. Clearly, the basic objective is to find usable, commercial ones.

Granted, we have to start out by just blasting away, but the end objective is meaningful ideas with which we can make money. This is rather different from "Oh gee! Let's just find a magic idea."

During the creative process of idea generation, we have to superimpose *reality*. We're not just saying let's come up with ideas, but rather let's come up with ideas that are *commercializable*.

It Takes a Process

In searching for ideas there must be some kind of a *process*. A process gives direction. Many companies try many times to come up with new products and business opportunities, but without some kind of a controlled approach to doing it—to find usable, commercial ideas—it just doesn't happen.

Without a disciplined process, it's the old "needle in the haystack" syndrome. Go out there. Look for ideas and hope you're going to find a good one. Maybe one time in a million you will find it. But those odds are far too high. You can't *plan* on finding that needle in the haystack. So you need a way of controlling the search; you need a process to help control where you're heading. Whether you are conducting chemical research, creatively generating new ideas, or starting new businesses, I believe some type of controlling process is absolutely necessary.

If you don't run your search within a rational process, usable results don't happen and many people get bent out of shape. Morale heads south because employees are working hard, creatively blasting away and coming up with a ton of ideas. But they see nothing happening as a result of their efforts. That's frustrating and a real morale downer.

Documentation Provides Feedback

An important part of any broad-based creativity session is to get all the ideas documented. People have to know you are recording them. More important, they have to feel you're going to *do* something with them. Oh, they'll come to one session, but this takes their time. Accordingly, they're going to lose interest if nothing comes of it. So, it's important to take the time to summarize everything that went on in that meeting and get back to everybody with "Here's the ideas that we all came up with, and here's where we're going with them."

You have to provide feedback—it will pay dividends. You just can't throw the output of their personal contribution—their "babies"—into a bottomless pit. Employees will come back again if you tell them what is going on.

Get out into the Market Immediately

You have to get out into the marketplace early. You can't do all of your development, even the idea generating, back in the laboratory, in the office, or in the meeting room. You have to hit the battlefield beaches.

For the products we launched from our program, we made thousands of phone calls, conducted thousands of interviews, and had hundreds of meetings with people in the outside world. Get out there and see what's happening. Get your feet in the mud. Get out there. Get on the shop floor and talk to the people. I believe strongly in that.

When I say we need usable, meaningful ideas, that's how you're going to get them—by being out in the marketplace at every stage of the process. By relevant ideas I mean ones relevant to the company, to the marketplace, and to the needs and trends.

The Critical Need to Stay Positive

I've hired people for thirty years and struggled to learn how to identify creativity in people. It's very difficult; there are no formulas. The key, if there is one, is to learn how to deal with this whole process.

And there's one other thing you absolutely must learn—and not waver from: *Be totally positive when creating ideas and never judgmental.* I'm absolutely sold on this point. Once you teach people the value of being positive, they become comfortable.

You just cannot be creative and evaluative at the same time. It is absolutely impossible. So we have to teach people the difference between these ways of dealing with ideas, particularly during the creative part of the process. We must teach people how to be positive—very positive—and show them how to separate creative idea generation from evaluations.

Executives are often highly judgmental and usually uptight with creativity. We know the story about the exercise with executives—giving them a piece of clay and saying, "Make something." They are very uncomfortable with that. What happens is they start asking questions. They start evaluating. But you just keep saying, "Do it!" Then they ask more questions, but you don't answer them. After about the fourth time, you say, "Just do it!" And they do. After maybe five minutes, they each create something out of their clay.

Then they are asked to evaluate their *buddy's* creation across the table, but they were cautioned before making any negative or disparaging remarks regarding the obviously and pathetically poor product. The point is that they are going to work with this guy for a long time and he needs to feel good about making suggestions. So their challenge is what to say about his "ugly baby." Somehow, that brings home the whole point of learning how to be positive in group meetings.

Another tool used to get the group to be positive is the "blue hat." Some blue baseball hats are passed out; the hats have lettered in front, "What's Good about It?" Everybody thinks that he or she is going to wear a blue hat so the others could constantly see the words. But the only person who has to wear the hat is the one who is negative. After the hat moves around two or three times, they get the message and nobody wants to wear that blue hat. It's unbelievable. That tool is so strong, that the blue hat becomes known throughout the corporation. We would sit at top-level management meetings that had nothing to do with new product generation and if anyone came up with a negative comment, the president or somebody else would say, "Give him the blue hat." So it works.

Being positive is very important to the overall process, because people— especially executives—are typically negative. They learn that almost everybody else is going to be negative. So they'll sit there in meetings thinking, "All right, how can I turn this guy around to get him on the positive side?"

The key is that first they learn how to do it to themselves. Second, they learn how to get other people not to be so negative.

Getting Started

You first need to generate specific criteria for the company, and it is imperative that top management accept these criteria. You should put a great deal of time and effort into this project at the earliest date. You absolutely need criteria, because when you go back to match the needs and trends you have identified in the marketplace with the resources that the company has, the list of criteria will be a guideline.

You should rework the criteria to make them realistic and then get top management to sign off on the list. After all this is completed, an idea that meets all of the criteria should, theoretically, be a good business opportunity and one your company will support.

In terms of generating and selecting meaningful ideas, you should have a list of around twenty criteria. The list won't be sitting in front of your face all the time, but in our case they were always in the back of our heads. So you need to work on them up front.

At the beginning of the overall process you have to say, "At this point we are not looking for new product ideas—that's our end goal, but when we start we have to *force* ourselves *not* to be looking for the end product." Everybody who's inexperienced at this *starts* by looking for the "magic new product idea," and they want it right now! You have to teach people to be patient, and that's part of what the controlled process does.

After a while, they understand that up front we are looking for opportunity areas. This is important because both individuals and groups want to focus on a product right away. They want to go to the answer; they look for the magic idea. It is natural, I suppose, because it happens all the time. We often hear, "Oh I've got a new idea. Here's a product." And we say, "Not now. Let's talk about opportunity areas first."

It works, but it takes a while for people to learn the concept and have the required patience. Make sure at the start you have broad areas that make sense.

After that, go out and look for needs and trends in the marketplace. At the same time, develop a list of real strengths of the company. Again, be realistic in assessing what your company is—or could be—really good at doing. Look for needs and trends in the marketplace; come back and look at what you are good at, then put the two of those together. If you do this well, you will have a dynamite end result. The ideas will be relevant because they're going to fit the criteria and the marketplace.

The Briefing Document

Next let's consider one of the other tools that is part of the process. The briefing document, which I've used many times, is something new to most people who have attended a creativity session. Some people have been to many different kinds of "brainstorming" meetings. They usually walk unprepared into the meeting, and somebody just expects them to blast away. It doesn't work well. You get some things, but not what you get in a more controlled process.

Accordingly, a lot of time should be put into this briefing document, and the recipients will be surprised and impressed. As a result, they'll typically put more effort into the work before they come. It will get their heads aimed in the direction you want before they even get to the meeting. Eventually, they'll see the value and logic of it.

They won't realize how controlled the session is going to be. In fact, that's a key issue. It *seems* like a wild free-for-all session, but if you do it right, it's tightly controlled. So work hard on that briefing document as the initial preparation for the meeting.

There are a number of different sections that should be in a briefing document. First, clearly write out the session objective. And, like they did in the military, tell them once, then tell them again later, and then later on in the document tell them what you told them. When you summarize, restate the objective again.

The objective should be broad. You want to tell them something like, "We're going to generate 200 ideas for such and such in an opportunity area." Maybe the second sentence would be a little more specific. Then you give them something specific to work on, for example, a list of questions that are broken down into different groups.

Some of the initial questions ought to be off-the-wall associations to get them to think beyond the conventional. For example, if they're looking at how to technologically improve the peel strength of a plastic weld, tell them to think about peeling an orange. Or what would happen if a lemon were frozen and you tried to take the skin off. Things like that. The tools and techniques shouldn't be too far away from home, too weird. It makes most people uncomfortable. If this happens, it makes the other tools, and the entire session event, suspect. It doesn't loosen them up. I think the way you loosen attendees is to give them things they can be reasonably comfortable with, but yet different from what they are used to.

Think about analogies in nature—how a bird holds onto a telephone wire, or how a barnacle attaches itself to rocks or even onto moving whales. If it's different, it's creatively useful. But there should be some rational tie-in. It's not just doing kooky stuff. I think most people—particularly where I've come from, dealing mostly with technological developments—are not the kind of folks that want to act like a dog or play with toys. It just makes them too uncomfortable.

So in the document and in a session, you take a number of different approaches that get them thinking differently but keep them headed towards the target at which you are aiming.

Assume you have a technology and you want your people to think about it in relation to the marketplace. You tell them a little bit about the technology, if that's needed. And you tell them some things going on in the marketplace. For example, the infrastructure in this country is starting to fall apart. The roads are crumbling, the bridges are in trouble, the sewer systems are in bad shape. There are some basic fundamental needs out there, and the government is starting, in some cases, to pump money into them. These are definite needs and definite trends.

What I'm getting at is that the briefing document should explain something like that to the participants before the meeting. Tell them there are these needs and trends out there and that we have some strengths that could address them. Ask them what we could do. Get them thinking. Ask them a few specific questions.

There are a few more things you can do. Put them to work before the session. Tell them to go look in some magazines. Tell them you're going to ask them certain questions and that they should think about some answers. That gets them headed in the right direction, gets them working on it before they come to the meeting. And it gets them convinced that it's going to be a meaningful and a fun meeting.

If you get them a briefing document beforehand, they'll work on it. They'll get themselves at least a little bit ready, and they'll get themselves interested. I've seen it happen. They all want to participate and contribute; they don't want all the other people coming with ideas. I've written many briefing documents and used many of the techniques, modifying them in different ways depending on the situation. That document is a valuable tool. I've had people come back to me and say, "You know I've been to many of these kinds of sessions, and I've never had anything like this to prepare me. Before I came, I had the feeling that this was going to be worth something."

Running the Session

It is important that the session be run by a skilled leader. He needs to know what he's doing. He needs to know that he has got to keep the group positive and keep them coming up with the ideas. Predesigning the session is important. Often, the participants are going to think that they're just sitting there and much doesn't make any sense, fit together, or lead anywhere.

But this attitude will not prevail if the leader has a plan before he gets there. He knows that he's going to talk about peeling the orange and then figuring out how those elements, insights, and ideas fit the strengths of the company. At another time, he's going to be exploring trends in the market-place, knowing full well that later he will direct the session toward combining the trends and needs ideas with the strengths ideas.

The leader needs a strategy, must be willing to control the session, and has to know where he's going. The participants don't. And you don't want them to. They don't want to *feel* like they are under any kind of control.

Sessions should not run too long. Usually a half-day session is typical of the way I've done it. They can run way beyond that, but sometimes you're forcing the effort. The leader has to make it clear that the objective is to generate ideas and pull them out of everybody as fast as he can, while being positive about doing it.

A mechanism is needed to write the ideas down to get them up in front of everyone. There are two approaches I like. A simple one is flip chart sheets tacked on the wall. Tape them all over the wall. It works great. People like to see their ideas up there.

The other approach is the white board. Cover the walls with those white boards you can buy in a lumber store and use colored markers to write all over the walls. We've lined whole rooms for almost no money at all. So cover the walls with them and write all over the room. It's different and dramatic, and it works. Then when people get loose, they'll jump up in the middle of a session, grab a pen and write somewhere. It works great because it keeps things up there for people to see. And there are many times they want to go back and say, "Wait a minute, I've got another angle on the idea that someone else had earlier."

Let each participant talk, but don't allow long monologues. Keep them positive throughout. Keep the whole meeting positive. Watch out for the "blue hat." Don't let anybody get negative.

Focusing Down

After the meeting, make sure that all the output is recorded and that some type of report is sent back to the participants. If you want them to come again, show them how you used their ideas. Write a report or summarize the output. This works in research; it works in everything.

People don't like to write reports, but I believe it's worth the effort to get it all down on paper. The main reason is that it's going to force you to organize. You're not just going to blast away when you have to report it on paper. And it will also induce intelligent questions. It is a mistake to leave a bunch of junk hanging around in an uncontrolled way, because in a few days it will be useless.

You've come to the next stage—you're in this funneling process. You must take some kind of approach toward narrowing down these opportunity areas. You can't work on everything. In this controlled process, you have to get yourself convinced that at some point in the process you will be required to narrow and focus your search—which means you'll have to throw things out.

The real world, as we've found it, is that people want to hang onto things and not let anything go. They are afraid to lose a good idea. This mind set must be changed. We tell them a baby *will* go out with the bath water once in a while. They've got to be convinced that even if it does, with a controlled process, they'll still have many other good ideas.

You need discipline. You can't work on a million ideas, or you'll get nowhere. We're playing with controlled odds. You have to think of it that way. And the disciplined, controlled process is going to help us beat the odds. It works. You must set some goals and say, "By x date we're going to have selected a specific number of opportunity areas." There's going to be a big battle over "Let's keep one more." But the process requires discipline to arrive at a focus. Without it, you're going to wander all over and get nowhere. Don't let it happen.

Using Outside Experts

We always bring in outside experts during the process because you can't know or even keep up with everything. Technology is moving around so fast, enterprises are growing so fast, and the marketplace is changing constantly. So it's always worthwhile to bring in outside experts for interviews or sessions. Outside experts can help with confirming needs and understanding how strong your strengths really are in the market. This will help to focus even more.

Finally, Looking for Specific Ideas

Now I think we're finally far enough into the process where you might want to start to look for some specific products. Use the same approach: get back to another creativity session. Use your own people if they know enough about the opportunity area, use outside experts if they don't, or even use both.

Tell them again about the marketplace, again about what's going on, again about what you found in the marketplace. Now say, "We're going to have a session directed at finding products to meet these needs and trends. How can we maximize our strengths in order to come up with specific products?"

From the output you might make some samples. Mock them up, fake them, but get something to look like the potential products you've identified. And get back out into the marketplace with them. Show them to people. Tell them they're mock-ups or a sample from the lab. But make them look something like what you're trying to get potential customers to understand.

Go everywhere; beat on people's doors. They'll love to talk to you. Tell them about the controlled creative process you've used. It gets them interested. Tell them how you arrived at your current point. They get involved and excited. Now that you've captured their interest, you can start to ask them questions. If they can't use the new product, they're probably going to want to work creatively with you, even if it's only for a short time. New ideas will come out of these meetings. You'll learn things.

You'll learn what's wrong. And you'll learn "What's good about it?" You'll learn what can be improved. But if you have that sample with you, it's so much more meaningful than going in and saying, "Hey, we've got this idea." Take the new product to the marketplace. That's critical.

Come back and refine your specific product ideas. Maybe even have another session with your group. Ask, "Does this meet the original criteria?" You've been thinking about that list all along, but check it out again.

Now you're down to what we wanted; coming out of this controlled process with meaningful, relevant ideas that can be commercialized, not just "ideas." Compare these usable ideas with your original criteria to be sure they still fit. And then take it from there.

ANOTHER VIEW FROM THE REAL WORLD

Raymond Wingard

Raymond R. "Randy" Wingard spent much of his career at the Koppers Company evaluating novel ideas. In the early 1980s he was one of the prime movers behind Kopvenco, the company's venture capital unit, where he served on the board for almost a decade. In this capacity he was part of a team that evaluated literally thousands of proposed startups—many founded on novel ideas—and he served on the boards of several small companies. So his experience comes from the perspective of both a large corporation and from working intimately with venturists themselves.

As a corporate vice-president and member of the future business planning team, Randy used INNOTECH's expert-to-expert sessions as an evaluation and decision-making tool to assess a number of new business opportunities under consideration. His experience with INNOTECH also includes generating criteria for Koppers and, ultimately, a mission statement to guide the company into the future.

He and several other top executives retired shortly after a protracted international battle resulting in the takeover of Koppers by Beazer PLC, headed by British industrialist Brian Beazer. Finally, Randy has also sponsored novel ideas outside of Koppers, and has generated some small businesses himself. He's never restricted himself to a single task, and today he is executive director of a national trade association. However, he finds time for consulting with Japanese industrial companies interested in U.S. investments, as well as for advising educational institutions on the cultural side of business.

Kopvenco was founded in recognition of the fact that people who are attempting to commercialize novel ideas more often than not need fast answers. They're not usually able to wait for a typical corporate board of directors to go through all of its gyrations. They really need answers quickly. Sometimes the need is financial, but not always. Frequently, it has to do with the personality of the individual who has the novel idea. He's so excited he can't wait to get on with it.

I believe that pride is one of the strongest driving forces behind commercializing new ideas. Those who do it want something to exist, whether they stay with it or not. They want to look back and say, "That wasn't there before, and it wouldn't be there if I hadn't done it." It gets down to a basic human need to change the world a little as a result of having been here.

When I look at someone who has a truly novel idea and wants to do something with it, I always try to find out what this person has done in his or her previous experience. Above all, I think a novel idea generator is a creative person who, like an artist, takes a blank canvas and creates something that didn't exist before.

Don't Start by Evaluating the Idea

When evaluating novel ideas, I believe that the best place to start is with the person or group that is presenting the idea, rather than with the idea itself. I start with trying to dig underneath. Has the person been creative before? Or is this just something he or she stumbled on in order just to make some money. There's nothing wrong with making money, but creative people are driven by something much more fundamental and important than that. General Dorio, the founder and president of American Research and Development, believed very strongly that you evaluated the people, not the plan. I know that many people believe that, but I'm not sure everybody looks at the *creative* side. I want to see if creativity has been at work inside of the individual's mind and heart, because that's the person who is going to give his whole body and soul to the venture. This answers the critical question of whether or not there is total dedication to this project. So from my perspective, it's important to evaluate the creative components and not just the business side. This will take some time. You won't be able to determine it in one meeting. It might take two or three weeks or a month to really get inside the person or group. All that time I'm trying not to evaluate the idea itself, because that will only get in the way at this point. Yet many people only evaluate the plan and don't even meet the entrepreneur. So when you have a group doing the evaluation, you probably need somebody who's purposely not looking at the business plan at this point. But you also need a hard-headed person who looks at the plan—and only the plan. So when you blend these views together you have the total picture.

At some point after I am satisfied that this person is totally dedicated to the idea for reasons other than just money, then obviously the idea has to be evaluated carefully in commercial terms. A person can be the most dedicated person in the world, but if he's marching in the wrong direction, he will still march off the cliff.

Don't Take the Plan Too Seriously

I've read and studied many, many business plans. Consequently, I don't believe they often express what is likely to happen or even what the idea generator really expects will happen. So business plans are a place to start—a kind of "vision" at the time. Usually, by the time an idea gets to a place like a venture capital board to be evaluated, a professional business plan writer has been hired. This plan says nothing about commitment; it just says that the proposing individual or group was smart enough to find a good writer. At least that says something about business sense. But except for the numbers, the plan is going to read just about like every other business plan you'll evaluate. We used to receive, and at least look over, something like forty a week when Kopvenco first got started. Later, this tapered off to around a dozen a week. They all looked pretty much alike. You could usually tell from the introductory paragraph whether the person or group had written it or hired a professional. Often the people who are going to run the business—the people who have the idea—have taken a back seat to the professional writer. They've become convinced that the business plan has to be presented in a certain format, has to read in a certain way, and has to cover how to generate a particular return on investment over a specific time period. So the plan will tell you what its proponents think you want to hear and will answer all the right questions. Yet the hit rate for business plans is significantly less than the success rate of startups, which is something like one in twenty.

Some Rules of Thumb

Based on all my experience, I've developed some principles or rules of thumb. One is to read or at least scan the business plan but then sit down with the people who have caused it to be written—the sponsors of the idea. Close the book and say, "I don't have any questions about the plan, it's a good one, but I'd like you to tell me in your own words what is it you're planning to do and why." My emphasis is more on the "why" than the "what." I don't think that at this point in time a new business really knows what it's going to do. But I like to hear why it is they think they want to do it. Does it fill a basic human need? Does it fill a gap in the marketplace? Is this so innovative that it is going to capture a large market share in a particular segment, in a corner of the world, or in the whole world? Is it a brand new idea, or is it built off a specific body of knowledge that has already been commercialized and is just waiting for the next step to be taken? So instead of studying numbers, you want to get behind the entrepreneur's vision and find out why he thinks this is going to succeed. He always has a vision; I've never run into one yet that didn't. But most people don't ask him about that. If he's really inspired and the idea itself makes sense in the marketplace, then you've really got something going.

Vision and Commitment Are the Keys

A good example of such a case was the startup of what was then called the American Robotics Company in Pittsburgh. Romesh Wadwahni is a graduate of Carnegie Mellon University. He's a top-notch scientist and an electronic technologist. When Romesh first came to Koppers to talk about his idea of super automation within the robotics industry, he impressed us greatly with his knowledge and his vision that the world really needed this. His number-one objective at that time was to become the supplier of robotic instrumentation to the Japanese—to beat them at their own game. Because his energy and dedication were so evident, he convinced us he would be able to do just that. The guy never sleeps. He's just a fantastically energetic and creative individual.

So we became one of the founding sponsors of his company, which is now known as American Cimflex Corporation. It has become a major player in robotics. Japanese and American automotive people have benefited because Romesh had the vision and energy to pioneer robotics instruments that can see and feel; his products have both sight and tactile capabilities. His robot arm can thread a needle a hundred thousand times over. He first inspired us with his vision and his commitment. Later we had to gain an understanding of the technology itself. Of course it was important, but we wouldn't have gotten to it had not the man's "vision" moved us so emphatically.

Get Expert Help!

Another point is that the idea evaluator or team is unlikely to be expert in the idea being evaluated. So there has to be a willingness to reach out and get experts to come in *after* you have decided this is worth further evaluation. They can educate you in the technology and sit in on the sessions where it's being evaluated. You really should have expert advisors, and they have to be the best. That's where the expert-to-expert sessions helped us in evaluating opportunities inside Koppers. In the past we'd frequently scan the academic world and find a researcher in whatever university that was doing the front-running research on the technology we were evaluating. We never found it a problem to get him in. We'd pay him, of course, but people like that aren't doing it for the money; they're doing it because it's their field and they're excited about it. So we'd use experts to help us evaluate new technologies that we were unfamiliar with—which was most of them.

The business plan can almost be on the back of an envelope, but in order to get it past most corporate committees, it's got to end up in a blue binder. It's often form over substance. But don't let the form take precedence over the substance—hear it from the lips of the inventor or the idea generator, not from the pen of a professional writer. Don't get fooled by a slick plan. And you'll want a real expert to help you on the technical side. But the "technical side" can be anything from art to science. If I were evaluating whether or not a new artist should be sponsored for an exhibition, I couldn't evaluate whether his art was significant. I'd need an artist to help me.

The Evaluator Needs a Passion for People

If someone is serious about becoming involved in the business of evaluating opportunities, he or she needs to be sincerely interested in what's going on inside other people. That's question number one, because you aren't going to spend the necessary time unless you have a sincere interest in the development of other people. Can you get your kicks out of seeing someone else succeed? Can you be satisfied to see someone else get all the glory from an idea that maybe, without you, would never have seen the light of day? If the answer is no, you really should stay off a team that's going to evaluate new ideas, because you'll be a detriment, not a help. What this game is all about is the development of *people*, not the development of *ideas*, because the ideas come from people. Entrepreneurs know that; but when you think about venture capitalists, you think of people who are just hard numbers oriented. They read the plan, they look at the numbers, and they seldom mention the people.

Don't Emasculate the Entrepreneur

One of the most frequent remarks you hear is, "Once we get this thing up and running, this scientist or idea generator is going to have to take a back seat." I don't agree with that. Yet it's frequently true that when a startup grows beyond the business knowledge of the inventor, you have to bring in a knowledgeable senior-level businessperson. But to have the inventor or idea generator report to that person is usually a big mistake. It normally should be the other way around. This just destroys the entrepreneur's creativity. You can call it ego if you want, but it just destroys the creative feeling inside of the person, which is what made it all work in the first place. It kills the drive, the commitment, and the enthusiasm.

I've seen this probably a dozen times at Kopvenco. When the first foray into the market didn't work—and it almost never does the first time—we said, "Well, the real problem is here; this guy's a scientist and not a businessman." And it's always a businessman making this decision. So we'd bring in a very high-powered guy, pay him twice as much as we'd ever paid the scientist, make him president or chairman of the company, and put him in charge. And we'd say to the entrepreneur, "Well now, you're still going to be the chief engineer, and it's your idea we're working on, but you're going to have to let this fellow call the shots about how to go to market." It destroys the people. You can see it in their faces. They agree because by that time they don't have a choice. At least leave the idea generator coequal with anyone else in the new venture. Coequal can work if they both understand it. But it's destructive to say to the person, "You're idea is great, but it won't sell because you just aren't smart enough to get it in the market."

It Takes Time to Be Honest

The next piece of advice I would give to someone evaluating novel ideas is be prepared to spend lots of time. Because you've got to understand what's going on inside the people and the business you're evaluating, it will take a far greater amount of time than you think. It isn't the first round of financing that is critical, it's the second, third, fourth, and fifth rounds. In order to be a part of that, you're going to have to spend enough time inside the minds and workplaces of these venturers to be able to sell other people on the venture. So my advice is don't accept any idea for investment that you would not recommend to your closest friend. If you can't do that, there's something dishonest about your own evaluation. You should be so excited about it that if there were an opportunity for a friend to invest, you'd be anxious to let him or her in on a good deal. So a rule of thumb is, if you can't recommend that a good friend get into it, something is wrong someplace.

It will help if you take the time to visit with some venture capital companies. Go and find out how they make decisions. Tell them you would just like to know what they're interested in and how do they go about their evaluations. You'll learn a lot that way. Some things you'll learn will be what *not* to do, because you'll hear, "Here are the things we've done that haven't worked out."

Can You Sell It in Your Company?

If you're looking at an opportunity strictly within a corporate framework—not as a venture capitalist—the first consideration has to be, Can you sell it to the company? Does it fit and make sense? How does this relate to the core business? Many companies only invest in those things that can eventually become a part of a core business or become a new core business. Question one would be, "What business could this be a part of in the future?" In order to determine that, you must have a good feel of where all your present businesses are going.

You're probably looking at a time horizon of ten to fifteen years for this idea to mature, so you have two moving targets. Your own businesses are moving and changing all the time, and this new business certainly is going to move and change. At some point in the future these lines could cross. And that's what you look for: Where is that crossing likely to occur, and what core business should it be a part of at that point in time.

Trying to examine a new business in a present-tense relationship to your current businesses is a serious mistake. Just as you look at money in terms of future value, you have to look at ideas in terms of future value. And a big mistake that I've seen many times is the corporate syndrome of "What will this idea do for me next year? . . . or the year after? . . . or in my three-year business plan?" And the answer is almost always going to be "Nothing." If you use that criterion, you won't invest in much. So you really have to look at future value and the intersect.

If you are inside a large corporation, you have to recognize that there are a lot of ideas that just won't sell internally for a host of reasons. Maybe a board member or a senior executive has been down this particular road and it didn't work out. Even though it might work now, you know that it's going to be opposed at high levels. So you'll only spin your wheels and waste time for the entrepreneur. The cardinal rule in the corporate game is to deal with reality. Whether or not it's a good idea, evaluate whether or not it truly has a chance in your company. It may be a wonderful idea, but it doesn't have a prayer of seeing the light of day in your particular organization. You'll do everybody a tremendous favor to sit down with the idea generator and tell him that, and maybe help him find someplace else to take it. Trying to sell it inside would be suicide for the idea. That could happen in any corporation for a lot of reasons not necessarily related to the merit of the idea.

Consider Human Resources

Make sure you have your venture capital activities slotted in the right function. For example, if it's in finance, it's unlikely to work, because the financial departments of large corporations have a totally different mission than that represented by venture capital. You need a financial specialist helping, but not as a part of the finance department. It can't be in the legal department either, because venture capitalists and lawyers are just like oil and water—they don't mix. You will need legal perspective for the team, but not as a formal part of the corporate law department.

I think venture capital efforts are fundamentally most directly related to the human resources function. That doesn't mean that the head of human resources is necessarily in charge of venture capital. But I believe that good human resources people understand the motivational influences that cause success; they understand it a lot better than financial or legal people. I personally feel it belongs to human resources more than any other part of the corporation, but I know how revolutionary this thought may be to most managers.

One problem may be that in some companies human resources work is viewed as a second- or third-level staff function. That can destroy the human resources value to venturers, inside or outside.

If that's true in your own company, you'll have to overcome it. It wasn't true at Koppers; human resources reported directly to the chairman. But if it's reporting three levels down, then maybe the best you can do is have the human resources director on the venture team. I would be sure he or she is there, because usually these are the only individuals who can really understand the people component—they're good "humanists." Admittedly, some human resources people are in that department because it was the easiest place to get into the corporation. But there are also a lot of really good, dedicated people in human resources because they want to be there. Those are the kind I'm talking about.

Introspection Required

Evaluating the ideas of others requires more self-evaluation than any other thing I have ever done. Remember, you really are dealing with the very substance of the lives and being of other people. Sometimes they're at that point where they could make a major leap that will change something on the human scene. So you have to be sure you've got your own mental house in order. You may find yourself lying awake nights wondering if you squelched an important idea . . . or are leading the way to World War III. You have to be sure that your evaluation is fair and objective, without irrational prejudices, because you're really evaluating a person. Evaluation of an idea requires tremendous introspection. You can't look at it as just another piece of your job. You have to look at it as the most important thing you're doing.

What You See Is *Not* What You Get!

We made around twenty or so investments in ventures that actually became small businesses. A few of them became large businesses, and three of them are listed on the major exchanges. Some of them have failed or have been absorbed by others. In all of them I observed one amazing thing: In no case did the business ever become what we expected it to be. More often than not, it served different markets or segments than originally intended. Somewhere along the way, for good and valid reasons, it took a right turn or a left turn. And I don't think our experience is much different from that of other people. So to think a company's business plan really describes what it's going to end up doing is naïve. Yet most people spend the most time talking about and analyzing that business plan. The business plan has all the things in it that businesspeople are accustomed to seeing. It has profit and loss projections and balance sheets. It has the things you can talk about to the third decimal point. I've heard heated arguments about whether the projection of a number that would apply fifteen years in the future was correct or incorrect. When this happened, I'd leaned back in my chair and went to sleep.

In reality, it's the resilience, vision, courage, and dedication of the driver that will make something happen.

7

RUNNING CREATIVE SESSIONS
How to Use Meeting Dynamics

Just as the three most important principles in real estate are
location location location, the three most important principles
in running a successful creative session are

1. *Preparation* (the right focus)
2. *Preparation* (the right participants)
3. *Preparation* (the right group dynamics and creative
   techniques)

Much of our discussion in this chapter fits under one of these
aspects of preparation.

CREATIVE SESSIONS HAVE GOTTEN BETTER

When most people think of a creative session, they think of
brainstorming. This seminal technique and the many principles
derived from it come from the work of Alex Osborn—the *O* of
the international advertising agency BBD&O. During the 1930s
Osborn made groundbreaking efforts in imposing some order
and quasi scientific rigor on the study of creativity.

Since the publication in 1953 of Osborn's *Applied Imagination*, we have made considerable progress in the techniques of creativity and group dynamics that go into running a successful creative session event. A well-designed, -staffed and -run session event today is to brainstorming what an F-16 fighter jet is to the *Spirit of St. Louis.*

Simply stated, brainstorming consistently underdelivers because of lack of preparation. A brainstorming session may have the right focus, but it seldom has the right participants, the right group dynamics, or the right creative techniques. Most often it's a gaggle of available people within an organization who merely toss out ideas. One of the biggest shortcomings is unrealistic expectations: the participants are expected to produce one or more "magic ideas," a pitfall we discussed in earlier chapters.

SESSIONS ARE ONLY THE BEGINNING

Even a well run session's true output is a lot of "white noise," which requires an enormous amount of work to filter and organize in order to turn it into valuable information. But this seldom happens. When no magic idea emerges, the session leader eventually walks away.

Seeing that nothing has resulted, the participants then lose their interest in attending the next event. Eventually, the session organizer loses interest in the session format itself as a vehicle for solving a problem or arriving at a new product or business opportunity. This is a classic example of throwing the baby out with the bath water. A well-staffed, well-designed, and well-run session is an extremely powerful tool that should be used more, rather than less, often.

What one can *realistically* expect from any session is a great deal of information, some insights, some ideas, some potentially helpful contacts, and the need for much work to extract the potential benefits. Expecting a session to produce useful results instantaneously is unrealistic, if not totally naïve.

TYPES OF SESSIONS

Today we recognize the limitations of brainstorming sessions, and we draw on different types of sessions. Sessions can be run for different purposes and, therefore, must be staffed and designed differently to maximize efficiency.

In the early 1970s we at INNOTECH did not realize this. Every session was a creative session, with the single purpose of producing creative ideas for new products. We then began to realize that some objectives were better served by conducting primarily information-oriented sessions.

We found this to be particularly true in looking for opportunity areas. In such a session the task is to identify both macro and micro trends, emerging technologies, and changes in market dynamics. All of these are then collectively processed into promising growth avenues to pursue. The information-oriented session is also the vehicle of choice for such tasks as assessing a technology or evaluating a potential acquisition.

However, when most people think of a session, they think of an event where creativity should be the modus operandi and the objective should be to produce ideas. This is exactly what's needed when a group is confronting a problem requiring a novel solution or when the task is to identify new products or businesses, but a different approach is demanded in many cases.

Sometimes we even find ourselves in a situation that requires both modalities—creativity and information—and it is possible to spend an appropriate amount of time pursuing both aspects. Staffing the right participants is the direct consequence of clearly establishing the objective and designing the session. Therefore, each type of session requires its own subtle or major variations and modifications.

The Expert-to-Expert Session

One type of session that we have developed and worked with successfully is what we call an Expert-to-Expert Session. We have mentioned these sessions in earlier chapters, and we discuss them at length in Chapter 8. Historically, sessions run in companies have almost always been staffed with internal people. On the other hand, the expert sessions INNOTECH ran were once staffed totally with outside specialists, because we had a strong bias against mixing internal and external experts. At that time we assumed there would be a negative influence by a client group that was so overly familiar with a problem that it lacked any semblance of objectivity. We were also concerned about how the presence of this group would affect the session leader. We felt that the downside of pressuring him or her in this way was not worth the risk.

Gradually over many years we were able to overcome these initial concerns and figure out the mechanisms for bringing together knowledgeable "experts" from both inside and outside into an effective event. The result has been nothing but good news.

Sessions as Preparation for Other Sessions

Another kind of session is one that functions as preparation or "briefing" for another group that will, in turn, have its own session. Many times an information-oriented session can precede a creativity-oriented session. The information-oriented group explores the relevant issues in depth to create the groundwork for a second group, which then will attack the task with a creative orientation.

So there are many types of sessions that can be designed around the specified objective. All should reflect careful staffing of participants, as well as the other steps needed to insure maximum productivity.

THE BRIEFING DOCUMENT

One of the most important tools for maximizing the productivity of any session is a carefully conceived, well-written briefing document, which is used to prepare the participants before they attend the session. The briefing document encourages both conscious and subconscious preparation. We find that the greatest benefit of the tools, techniques, and exercises embodied in it are not what the participants bring to the session in their documents, but the effect the preparatory work has in infiltrating their subconscious minds and enhancing their creative productivity in the session itself.

This preparation often includes motivating a participant to discuss the subject with associates. This can contribute additional relevant knowledge to the participant's existing store. The briefing document also can suggest that the individual bring in relevant literature from books or periodicals in his or her area of expertise. Encouraging participants to bring in samples—often especially relevant on a program to find applications for a material—can result in a roomful of valuable artifacts.

A useful technique that often triggers creativity in an individual is to enclose cash along with the briefing document and suggest that the participant go shopping for items in a particular category. This most often applies to sessions that will have a consumer orientation.

Some general guidelines can help you create a briefing document. First, you must communicate the needed information and tailor it to the task. There is a danger of getting lazy and letting documents become fairly standard. Although some sections may lend themselves to standardization, it is worth the effort to design each document for the particular session.

Try to make it fun! Don't hesitate to use pictures, visuals, games, or matching columns. Your objective is to provide thought-provoking stimulation to the participants. When appropriate, don't hesitate to be abstract. Certain types of sessions, such as those aimed at a specific technical problem, work better when analogies and other similar techniques are used, instead of going at the task literally—"head-on."

Creative Techniques in Briefing Documents

One source of analogies useful for stimulating creativity is nature, but with imagination you can find them anywhere. For example, years ago, in the early days of introducing nonwoven fabrics, we were working on the task of coming up with new, improved ways to promote desired orientations and, thus, greater strength.

Rather than going at this task head-on using microscopic fibers, we felt it would be creatively useful to disguise the true problem. So the briefing document gave the participants the task of conceiving of new ways of orienting logs in a river so they could be more effectively and automatically transported up a conveyer into a sawmill for processing.

The session participants quickly devised various techniques that would use the readily apparent great mass of the logs to strike each other in order to achieve desired orientations. The various proposed systems and baffles were ingenious and promising. Midsession, however, the participants were told the real problem, and the task became to use these same "inventions" to manipulate the microscopic fibers.

Now, their already heightened creativity knew no bounds, and several promising approaches resulted based on the newly "discovered" mass of the microscopic fibers. Many or most of the proposed ideas probably would not have been generated had the true problem not been disguised, thus allowing the mass of fibers to be viewed as a useful tool.

Other Uses of the Briefing Document

A key benefit of a carefully designed, well-written briefing document is that it captures the attention of the participants, giving them the feeling that this is going to be a special event and not just another off-the-wall brainstorming session. Also, the contents inserted into the document before they even arrive is sometimes extremely valuable. Keep in mind that the participant is typically working with the briefing document in her office or home and, therefore, is surrounded by, or can easily access, her literature, reference works, and samples.

For one session a participant showed up with a prototype of an idea he had that was stimulated by the briefing document. The objective was to have participants conceive of a new approach to controlling sound patterns at a concert-type event where the live audience and shape of the hall would play dynamic roles. The participant had a compelling interest in the problem and had been trying to develop a computer program to simulate the components of it for a number of years. This base of knowledge allowed him to conceive of an approach to address the task and actually put together a crude prototype to demonstrate his idea. Thus, a briefing document can be extraordinarily valuable.

SESSION MECHANICS

Time

Just as sessions can be designed for a variety of objectives, so they also can be planned for varying lengths of time. Typically, a session will be a half-day, morning event, preferably on Tuesday through Thursday. This schedule works well because a well-designed and well-run session can be intense and extremely tiring for both the leaders and participants. Few individuals work or think for a prolonged period at the demanding level of intensity a session demands.

An oft-heard comment from a first-time participant leaving a session is, "Wow, I'm exhausted." Another common remark is, "That was really fun." And the third, and most telling, is, "I can't believe I had so many ideas because I thought I'd exhausted myself on the briefing document before I ever got here." Running the event in the morning is simply to exploit the fact that most people are mentally freshest then. Also, they haven't spent a half day in their normal roles dealing with their normal problems and distracting themselves from the task of the upcoming session.

Finally, we have found from experience that Mondays and Fridays are not the best days to conduct sessions. It seems that many people need a Monday to get back up to full speed after a weekend. Fridays are often more inconvenient for travel, and sessions can run late. Many people also begin to wind down mentally for the weekend.

There are reasons to vary this format. If a session is to be informational (this type of session typically is not as intensive or draining), more time may be valuable. Information sessions can run a full day, with an eat-in lunch break.

Another format that we have found productive is to have a "mini" warm-up session the evening before the full session, but run at a much lower level of intensity. The objective here is simply to get the participants to meet each other and to begin thinking about the following day by walking them through a few simple exercises in a limited time. This has the great benefit of getting the event off to a flying start the next morning.

The Room

Because the room in which the event is held can have a positive or negative impact on the session, its selection should not be taken casually. One of the things we've learned about rooms and their effect on dynamics is that they should not be too large. If they are, a sense of intimacy, which is a plus, is lost.

Sources of distraction should be eliminated. These can range from a window overlooking a crowded swimming pool to the noise of hammering in the adjacent room.

The Table

The configuration of the table and the seating arrangements are very important. A round table is ideal, but not always available. If it isn't, the closest configuration that can produce a square is the next best alternative. The worst one is the classic long, narrow board table where it is impossible to maintain eye contact with all the other participants.

What we are trying to achieve with such physical structure is a feeling of participation, intimacy, or team spirit. Another important factor is maintaining a comfortable temperature, because extremes can interfere markedly with the running of the session. We remember an internal session held in PPG's headquarters in Pittsburgh during the debugging phase of their new Crystal Palace. Occupancy had just begun, and the session, being held in January, was severely handicapped by the fact that everyone ended up in overcoats and gloves!

Wall Space, Chairs, and Room Size

Wall space is critical for displaying the session's work products, that is, the flip chart sheets. All too often, however, most of the wall space is unusable. Try to find a room that provides ample usable wall space for posting and work. If a room is to be specially set aside or designed for sessions, it is desirable that it have the capacity to handle slides, overhead projectors, and audio—both coming in and going out.

Avoid chairs that are too soft and comfortable. Instead, select ones that will help promote alertness. This may not be as true if an individual is being personally creative.

OBSERVERS?

The subject of whether nonparticipants should be allowed to observe a session is controversial. The normal bias coming from the session leaders is against the practice. Arguments include that the mere presence of observers may have a negative effect on the group dynamics and team spirit. Also, if an observer has not undergone the same preparation as the participants, he or she will not be as knowledgeable about the session's subjects and objectives. Because observers' normal tendency is to judge, another drawback is that their snap judgments can have a negative impact on the session.

If the decision is to have one or more observers, it is far better that they not be in the same room or even visible to the session participants. A classic solution is the one-way mirror often used to observe focus groups. Now the observers can be involved in the "feeling" and dynamics of the session but unable to exert a negative impact with their comments or even body language. Another approach that may be more practical is to install a television camera and transmit the session to another room where observers are encouraged to have creative discussions among themselves.

One benefit of having a problem owner as an observer is that he or she can provide midsession feedback to the session leader. This feedback can be suggesting new areas to explore based on insights derived from the session or having the group reconsider a promising area that could profit from more exploration and creativity. However, an observer's primary job—and toughest challenge—is to contribute his or her own creativity and information to the session while remaining nonjudgmental. Also, being an observer of a session better qualifies an individual to participate in the postsession guidance of the debriefing process. Unquestionably, the "right" observer with the "right" attitude can be a definite plus, but satisfying these two requirements is sometimes difficult.

THE ACTUAL SESSION

As already emphasized, designing and strategizing the session—beginning with its prime objective or objectives—are critical steps, because from these will flow the logic for the selection of participants. Assuming the proper staffing and a good briefing document, the final task is to take the total available session time and allocate blocks of it to the various themes and subjects that will be explored. By this time the planners should know which specific techniques will be used in each area to elicit creativity or information. However, the leaders will not know all the answers before the session begins, so the design should include a midsession break to assess what's happening and make any necessary course corrections.

Any subject area included in a well-designed, well-run session will elicit comments and participation from all attendees. Consequently, it may make sense to select the primary objectives carefully and limit the session to a thorough, in-depth exploration of a selected few—generally, three to five—subject areas. This is not a hard-and-fast rule but only a suggestion that might be helpful in wrestling with the design of sessions.

We have found that providing appropriate stimuli is an excellent way to trigger insights and ideas. One technique we have found helpful, depending on the session's focus, is aural triggers. We've used appropriate music, industrial or domestic noises, and even nature sounds that help create the right environment. Their benefit should not be overrated, however, because the right staffing, briefing document, and techniques are most important.

Visual stimuli seem to offer a more direct approach. These can be something as simple as key words written on cards and attached to the wall. We've seen some individuals take these words and construct a mobile "sculpture" suspended from the ceiling over the table. Product samples placed on the table are also effective in triggering ideas and insights.

Putting a 35 mm projector on automatic and flashing shots of various domestic scenes can be useful in a consumer product session that focuses on the home environment. The same is true for an industrially oriented session and environment. Thus, depending on the objective of the session and the creativity of the leaders, these stimuli can be highly productive.

Getting Started

When two dogs meet for the first time you can expect a certain amount of "nose rubbing."

When you bring together a group of bright and powerful individuals, you can expect at least as much. Therefore, you must allow time for personal introductions. Sometimes, however, these introductions can consume an inordinate amount of time. To prevent such delays, the leader can collect biographical comments ahead of time and introduce each participant. This certainly assures a high degree of control, but it's better if the individuals introduce themselves. However, they should be reminded that there is a time limit (two minutes is normally a sufficient span), and the leader should set the example by delivering a prototype introduction.

If the group is comprised of individuals who will be compensated for their participation (e.g., outside experts), we recommend distributing the checks *before* the session starts. This seems to make the individuals feel a little more obligated to perform.

Rules for the event should be clearly delineated by the leader. In his or her introduction, the leader should also strive to remove any fear of potential criticism from the minds of the participants. Introductory remarks should also encourage laughter and lightness.

We have used the following set of guidelines since 1969. They are lettered on a one-way mirror, and many participants and visitors have asked for a copy.

1. Defer judgment and think positive!
2. A new idea is a combination of known elements, i.e., $A + B + \ldots n \rightarrow C$
3. Really let your imagination go. The objective is lots of ideas (quality is a function of quantity).
4. Sketch each idea on a card, then add a few words, your initials, and the date.
5. Expose your ideas to others and contribute to the other people's ideas.
6. Don't overdevelop an idea.
7. Watch out for subgroups.
8. Let the leader worry about parameters.

9. Don't get tense.
10. Relax, laugh a lot, and enjoy yourself.

Some Principles and Techniques

Probably the single most important thing a session leader can do to enhance the productivity of a session is to provide a great deal of positive feedback. Participants tend to offer their ideas and insights tentatively at first, so the sooner they gain the confidence that positive feedback provides, the sooner the session will start to take off.

In designing the session, try to run those exercises that are aimed at individual contributions first. For example, one way to start a session is to have each participant complete a task by writing on a large sheet of paper posted on the wall. A physician might write down the types of operations he or she has performed; an engineer, classes of mechanisms; a psychologist, ways to make people comfortable. The objective later in the session may be to creatively integrate all these into new therapeutic chair configurations.

One principle that applies to a wide range of creative techniques is to establish quotas or goals for each exercise. These are embodied in quantity and time parameters. For example, the leader might say, "In the next two minutes come up with twenty uses for a brick." This framing of the assignment creates pressure and competition, which help get the participants into a quantitative, rather than qualitative, thinking mode. Done with a group, it also ensures a wide range of coverage on the assignment. In the words of INNOTECH's services division president, Kurt Eastman, "Keep the heat on 'em."

Keeping the heat on tends to raise the level of adrenaline in the group and results in a higher level of creative energy. A leader who is sitting comfortably in his or her chair and casually instructing an overly comfortable group is going to run a low-intensity and, probably, poor session devoid of many insights or ideas.

A simple technique for further enhancing the creative energy and, to a small degree, the pressure of competition, is to group individuals into two-person or even three-person teams. There is the internal competition among the team members and then the broader competition of team versus team, all generating ideas, insights, or solutions. This approach is best used after the dynamics of a session have already developed. However, utilizing it for more than half an hour tends to lower its potential benefits.

To Diverge or Converge?

One thing to keep in mind is that sessions can be run divergently or convergently. Being creative and exploring new avenues as they emerge lead to divergent thinking. Left alone long enough, a creatively led and highly motivated group may end up anywhere—probably quite a long distance from the intended target.

Convergence involves that phase where things are pulled back into focus and rationally redirected. Sessions with a creative objective are heavily divergent—sometimes involving little or no convergence. Thus, convergence must often be handled through the subsequent activity, debriefing. In contrast, information-oriented sessions tend to be far more focused, so convergence is often a planned feature. The decision about which mode to use is the session leader's. If the leader is happy with what he's getting, and has the time to spend in the area, he should continue to allow the session to "happen."

Assuming that the participants have spent several hours exploring the areas identified by the briefing document, it is often a productive exercise to save a small amount of time at the end for convergence. One closure technique we often use is what we term the CEO exercise. Simply, the participants are told that they should play the role of the CEO of the unknown sponsoring company, and in this frame of mind, identify a specified

number of the most promising ideas or areas they would personally want to "bet on" and pursue. The result can be a high
degree of congruence among the participants—or none at all.
In any event, this exercise provides the session leaders with
some starting directions for their subsequent debriefing analysis.

The Session Leader

Typically, the skill and experience of the session leader are
major factors in the success and productivity of the event,
because he or she must often redirect the happenings. At other
times, however, the leader's greatest contribution is to stay out
of the way of a highly motivated group that gets off to a flying
start and stays on target. Techniques or tools to enhance the
productivity of the event are not ends in themselves. If the
group is being highly creative and productive, don't wake them
up to take their creativity pill.

Sessions should have two leaders: (1) a primary leader to
introduce the techniques and steer the session and (2) an assistant leader to make sure ideas and insights are documented,
enabling them to serve as triggers for subsequent ideas and
insights. The assistant leader also can be a bit more dispassion-
ate and objective in monitoring the interpersonal relationships
and general dynamics of the session itself.

The leader should clearly keep in mind that the goal of
the session is quantity—again, Osborn's first principle—because
this will usually lead eventually to quality. As the prime objective of the session is generation of ideas, time set aside for
evaluation is the exception rather than the rule. Only the most
information-oriented session could justify using more than 20
percent of the total time for analytical thinking.

To help create energy and excitement that will enhance productivity, the leader has to be in top form—physically and emotionally. It helps, too, for the leader to bring drama, movement,
and valuable humor to the flow of events. A critical attribute is

that he or she have outstanding listening skills, because through effective listening the leader can catch clues or insights that can creatively refocus the session and lead to its best output. If the leader cannot control the flow and dynamics of the session, he or she may find that much of the time was wasted on exploring and intellectualizing areas irrelevant to his or her mission.

Controlling the Session

When the leader decides that he or she has gotten the desired results from a particular exercise or area, he or she must have the skills and discipline to move the group on to another area. Failure to do this results in the normal tendency to overdevelop a particular idea that turns the group on. The participants would happily play with a single idea and develop it for hours rather than set it aside and generate others that could have equal or even greater potential.

Clearly, the best way of positively controlling a group is not to tell any particular individual to stop talking. The most effective and simplest tool we have found for achieving the same result is to publicly recognize an individual's contribution and ask him or her to write it down on a notecard. The leader can then encourage another participant to talk.

One of the hallmarks of an INNOTECH session event is that the participants are armed with 4 X 6 cards on which to jot their ideas, insights and information. At the same time this provides the main vehicle for controlling the dynamics of the session.

The ultimate, last-resort technique for dealing with an individual who is totally disruptive in a session—by being either totally negative or unbearably dominating—is simply to have someone come in and announce, "There's a telephone call for you." When the individual leaves the room to take the call, he or she is asked to continue the process of leaving—completely. Fortunately, this tool is seldom required.

Figuring out What Happened

As stated earlier, expecting a session in and of itself to produce useful results is unrealistic. Sessions need to be followed by *debriefing*. This simple word describes a number of activities requiring significant time and effort in order to analyze, understand, supplement, and research the session's output. All this is required to turn the hundreds or even thousands of bits and pieces of information, ideas, insights, samples, and articles into information and insights that are truly useful to the event's sponsor.

Debriefing is hard, time-consuming work. Without it, however, a session's output would be virtually useless. So the fourth and least aspect of "preparation" is preparing the output of a session—a session for which the planners took so much valuable time to find the right focus, the right participants, and the right group dynamics and techniques.

ANOTHER VIEW FROM THE REAL WORLD

John Knapp

When John Knapp became involved with INNOTECH's Planned Growth process, he was president and CEO of an ITT company providing specialty fasteners primarily to the building construction market. He was the sponsor of a growth program to move the company's skills and strengths into related areas, and he was intimately involved in all the creative events and exercises conducted with his management team.

John has taken the knowledge and skills acquired in that program, creatively tailored the "tools" to other situations, and used them successfully in a wide range of challenging real-world situations. He is currently group vice president of Bowman Distribution, headquartered in Cleveland, Ohio, a subsidiary of The Barnes Group.

Keep Creative and Critical Thinking Separate

The major force behind our program to develop new ideas was *creative-*thinking sessions. Then we had *critical-*thinking sessions to take the resulting ideas and examine them in the light of reality to see which ones made sense and which didn't. Next we tested them against some things we had done in the past in order to come up with a plan of attack.

I have always used the technique of creative- and then critical-thinking sessions—and story boarding—to solve problems in my business. This approach is a powerful way of addressing a wide range of problems.

There has to be a distinct time gap between sessions using the two mental modalities because they are so different. Stop the creative-thinking process at the point where you have gotten all the ideas you can get. Sometimes, all it takes is a coffee break. Your objective is to change gears and put on the critical-thinking hat.

Story Boarding

To get some kind of "envelope" or structure around the event, I like to use what I call "story boarding." In a creative session we put the ideas on three-by-five cards. Then when you get a whole bunch of these, you take a break and start organizing them into natural groups and categories, and then you put a header card up describing each category.

Another approach is that the facilitator or leader starts the meeting by establishing some header cards. This puts some thoughts in the participants' minds. So for me it has worked effectively either way. You kind of free form the ideas and then see how they break out. Or maybe you get some header cards and ask the people to generate some ideas in these particular categories. As you go into it, you tend to get natural subdivisions, so one header card may subdivide into two or three more areas. Since every session event is a little bit different, you have to let it flow and see what happens. Don't put any artificial boundaries on it. That's where creative thinking comes in—you can't be rigid. You've got to let it flow, let it go where it goes.

Use Idea Cards

It's critical to get the ideas captured in writing, and I think cards are best. Of course, you can also use large scratch pads and felt-tip pens. But with cards, you can manipulate them easily throughout the process. Cards lend themselves to manipulation.

After you get a bunch of ideas down and categorized, you can start thinking about testing them against what you are attempting to do. That's the "gear switching" into critical thinking. As mentioned before, that can take place immediately after a small break, or it can take place a couple of days or even a month later. I don't feel there's a time constraint.

Benefits of a Group Process

About the critical-thinking side, when I was starting my career and was just getting into my first management job, I had a "macho" attitude. I personally had to be the one to generate all the ideas and come up with all of the programs.

Then after years of managing people I guess I got smarter. I came to realize that there is a tremendous amount of creative talent locked up in all people. If we could somehow extract it, we would certainly be better off than attempting to come up with all of the ideas ourselves. I've embraced the group process in my business, and I use it for just about everything we do, because I know *I* really don't have all the ideas.

Use Your Inside Experts

For close-to-home problems, people that are intimately familiar with what they are doing and have worked with it for a long time are the ones that potentially could come up with terrific ideas. So if we can get the right talent, and all the ideas in the back of their heads, together in a room and unleash them, we're going to be far more likely to come up with some really good ideas and solutions than with one individual sitting down at his or her desk and trying to think through all the alternatives.

I don't mean to say that as a manager of a business you abdicate your responsibilities. You definitely have to be personally involved. In the creative-then-critical process you often come up with a number of alternatives that make sense. So somebody has to select the winners and make some decisions. But in making that decision, you have incorporated the experience and wisdom of the group and put forth a lot more alternatives than you would have thought of yourself. As a result of all that, you probably have a better array of alternatives from which to make the decision as to which course you are going to take.

Of course, when you do have the alternatives pretty well narrowed down, you can enlist the group's help in making the decision. You should consider their advice and counsel, but in the end it's your decision, because you're responsible for it.

Team-Building Benefits

There is another important aspect of what we have discussed. Once you get people involved in the process, you are building a team. The mere fact that you would ask a group of your people to come in and help attack a problem by creatively and analytically thinking it through gets their involvement. They must feel much better about it all by the end of the day. It's an invaluable team-building tool. They feel they are a part of the whole process because they really are, and that's an extremely important aspect.

The Leader

One of the most important things to do is have a facilitator run the session. His or her job is to make sure that the group doesn't get too far off track. A good session leader can't be rigid, because one of the things you want is a free flow of ideas. But you can't let it get so far off track that you are not going in the direction you want.

There has to be a modicum of control exercised by the session leader. The reins have to be held loosely. But when the time comes to make sure this powerful team goes in the right direction, you have to tighten up a bit.

The Briefing Document

I think briefing documents are invaluable. Whenever you get into meetings that involve creative and critical thinking, you must have some envelope within which to start. Briefing documents can give a good starting point. If you are running a meeting where you don't have one, the leader has to come up with some background information that will put the problem into perspective so that all the participants will be operating from a common benchmark.

Another valuable aspect of the briefing document is that when the participants get it ahead of time, their subconscious starts to ruminate on the problem. If you deliver the information just before the session event, you might get them focused, but you haven't had the benefit of the "cooking" time. When people use it correctly, their creative juices start flowing and it makes the session more productive and efficient. It certainly allowed us to generate more ideas.

The Value of Outside Experts

Outside experts in a meeting can contribute information your people don't already have. When we were running through the process at Phillips Drill, the experts would come in with a number of ideas and suggestions that we had an opportunity to explore. Each one of these provided invaluable information to the process. If we can have a common starting point, a common benchmark, such as the information the experts bring, this flows in the direction of making the meeting as productive as possible. In fact, the critical thinking sessions we had at Phillips were long, hard debates on each of the alternatives the experts had brought up on our project.

The Value to You and Your People

One really good example of the word *synergy* is creative thinking, because one plus one truly does equal five. There is so much power in getting a group of people together and getting their ideas on the table that you truly do have synergy. Second, no one of us has a lock on all of the knowledge in the world. A manager running a significant business really needs the expertise and knowledge that rest with the people who have to do the job.

When I sit and ponder a decision, I'm so much better off if I have had an opportunity to tap into that knowledge power of my people, to sit down and get their ideas and alternatives on the table. I couldn't operate in an environment where I just had to sit down and think about our problems and come up with all the ideas myself. I'd feel like my arms and legs were tied.

I've also learned the value of the team-building aspect of this process. It's been my experience that almost 100 percent of the people really want to get involved, really want to contribute, and really want to feel good about what they are doing. I think some managers have the misconception that people tend not to want to contribute. I believe the opposite, and by getting them involved, you are going to be building a team. Also, you are going to be unleashing some of that creative power that is in everybody. The result is that you will be building more productive people and a more productive organization.

I've participated in about 150 creative sessions of all kinds. Some of them were small—two or three people putting some ideas on the chalkboard. Others have stretched over days where we tackled some major issues. In the latter category, we have recently put together a focused strategy for Bowman Distribution. That whole process was developed through creative- and critical-thinking sessions. Our mission—the unique factor and driving force—and agreement on our key strategies both came from that.

8

OPTIMIZING EXPERTS
How to Get Originality from
Employees and Consultants

For our purposes, an expert is someone who has spent considerable time and energy gathering information and gaining experience in a particular area. Axiomatically, he or she knows more
than we do or *we* would be the expert. Given this fact, we can
profit from the judicious selection and effective use of such
individuals who can help us get smarter faster, contribute to our
new business development planning, and help with the implementation of important actions.

AN EXPERT IS . . .

We classify experts into two categories:

1. *Inside experts* are those individuals within our own business
   unit or, more broadly, our corporation.
2. *Outside experts* are all others. We most often find them as
   consultants, suppliers or customers, academics, editors or
   writers, trade organization representatives, or government
   agency employees.

We tend to use inside experts when the problem or subject we are addressing is close enough to home to be within their knowledge and experience base. Clearly, if we are dealing with a variation on a theme or an improvement to an existing product or service, we would be well advised to rely in large part on our internal expertise. Outside experts are called on in situations where we are dealing with areas beyond the purview of our organization's existing "human data base." Making this distinction clearly can allow us to select wisely where to go for specialized knowledge, rather than assuming that "we should always use our own people" or that "we should always go outside and find the best experts we can."

We will assume that, except for special cases, an organization is well aware of its existing knowledge and centers of excellence and has a culture and the supporting mechanisms to allow effective use of these resources. However, the larger an organization, the less true this tends to be. Because of sheer numbers of personnel, mechanisms beyond informal networking are often required, especially when individuals can come from different facilities that are geographically quite far removed.

Why Use Outside Experts?

Many managers oppose the use of outside resources because, in their view, they already have thousands of highly qualified people. If the expert session will be directed to the company's core business or a closely related area, outside experts may not, in fact, be needed. However, we believe that any such session is enhanced by the objectivity and new information that outsiders bring.

Gaining Fresh Insights. Because everyone in the company already has a full-time job supporting today's businesses, they cannot be faulted for not taking time away from current responsibilities to scan a large and busy world for promising trends and changes. Even recognizing that, we didn't believe, when we began our activities, that large, seemingly successful companies could have significant knowledge gaps in areas critical to their businesses. Since then, we have been shocked on many occasions.

A good example might be an American company that is the leader in the field of simple, energy-storing mechanical products. During the course of a program to identify new growth areas, the top management group selected one area as particularly interesting. Moving further into it, we learned that the potential "new product" had already made significant inroads into their business and had taken nearly 20 percent of their market share on their most profitable product line for the past two years. Yet top management had not been aware of this development! They had, however, heard of the product, and they felt that *someone* in the company must be on top of the development. When we met with that someone, the opposite was true. Finally, in researching the area, we visited some of the distributors who were carrying the product and selling it in direct competition with our client's. All this had occurred despite the fact that our client must be considered a sophisticated, well-managed company.

We've run into dozens of cases like this where a company's lack of knowledge in a closely related area, or even in its core business, is surprising, if not appalling. So outside experts can play the role of bringing to the surface objective, unfettered, unbiased, unpleasant information quickly and efficiently. Bringing a half dozen or so carefully selected and prepared specialists together in an open session is a powerful tool that management should consider.

Keeping the Sponsor Secret.   One benefit of using outside experts is that by taking some pains, the name of the sponsoring company can be kept confidential. There are some obvious benefits in this. One is that the company's interest in a particular area is kept confidential. Second, it is amazing how much of a disruptive effect a stereotyped viewpoint of a company will have on its efforts to solicit fresh thinking.

For example, we've often said that if a group of participants were brought together and given the task of generating new product ideas for Gillette, chances are that most participants would come up with ideas and suggestions around shaving. This core image can clearly be a detriment when the organization's objective is to encourage fresh, unbiased thinking that will move it beyond its existing products.

WHERE TO FIND THE EXPERTS

Identifying the appropriate experts to bring together in order to represent adequately the needed market and technical areas is a creative exercise in itself. We frequently hear the question, "Where do you get your experts?"

Outside Experts

Among the excellent resources are the staff at universities that have centers of excellence in the desired area. Another—which we believe is underutilized by businesses—resource is the many editors and writers of various trade magazines and technical publications. These founts of knowledge may have just completed a survey or roundup article on an area of interest, and they are gatekeepers on stories and releases describing new products or technologies. There are also legions of trade and professional organizations who sometimes have impressive and knowledgeable staff members eager to serve their group or industry. Retired executives, government agencies, potential suppliers, or customers are also candidates for an invitation to an expert session—provided that there are no conflicts of interest.

Inside Experts

If internal experts will be involved occasionally or frequently, it makes sense to spend the time, effort, and money to set up a mechanism for cataloging them. Because each participant brings all of his or her knowledge and experience, as well as professional expertise, to the session we also catalog avocational interests. After all, ideas are the products of everything that an individual knows, and many insights come from private-time pursuits.

If a company can build its own "brain bank," this can be a helpful tool throughout the organization. In most companies such a data bank doesn't exist, so there is seldom any interchange among disparate areas, particularly among units such as divisions or entities that are locted in distant geographical areas.

WHY EXPERTS COME

Imagine an individual who has spent a significant portion of his or her life learning everything possible about the osmotic properties of toad membranes or about the aerodynamics, drift angles, and densities of snowfall. Not too many people are vitally interested in either subject. Therefore, when experts are asked to share their valuable expertise, they generally feel flattered and eager to display their knowledge and participate in an event where they would be among the stars.

Many times the expert has been identified and recommended by one or more peers. In fact, a thorough attempt to staff a particular area of expertise will often lead to the pinpointing of a specific person by a number of people. Given such recognition, the identified expert feels motivated to live up to the advance billing. This may account for the fact that invited experts—no matter what the level and stature of their reputation—will put in a number of hours on the briefing document prior to the session.

DETERMINING THE TYPES OF EXPERTS

Coming from the premise that "all of us are smarter than one of us," the session format allows us to design and build a collective superintellect in the area under exploration. We contend that in today's fast-paced, complex world, the Renaissance man who knew everything is an impossibility. The explosion of information occurring in every field forces practitioners toward increased specialization.

The fact that a well-led session can accommodate seven or eight specialists gives one the luxury of actually designing the contemporary analogue to Leonardo da Vinci or Benjamin Franklin. So the fundamental principle in staffing such an event is to cover the objective thoroughly from every angle.

An important issue that needs a conscious decision is whether or not to have more than one individual represent an area of expertise. If the session's objective is creativity, experience says that the dynamics will be better if each individual singularly represents his or her area of expertise. More than one individual with the same knowledge base can lead to arguments, overcompetitiveness, and generally poor session dynamics. On the other hand, if the objective of the session is primarily informational, it is a plus to have more than a single individual represent an area of interest, because this builds in the checks and balances that keep an individual from indulging in flights of fancy.

Interestingly, in staffing individuals for a session event there is a certain component of self-qualification. If the planners emphasize not just money as the reason for participating but also the benefits of interacting with other interesting people and participating in a unique event, only the "right" people will tend to want to participate. (This becomes even more true when the honorarium for participation is purposely kept rather modest.)

Staffing a "Wild Card"

Approaching a task conventionally by employing mainline areas of expertise is powerful and effective, but a session can be greatly enhanced by the presence of a "wild card." This is an expert who knows nothing of the actual area being explored in the session but who, because of his or her background, can bring fresh and objective perspectives to the quest, which can serve as triggers to the other participants.

Many times the wild-card role is filled by individuals who come from the natural sciences, especially those under the broad umbrella of "biology." For examples, we have worked with an individual who was the world's authority on the shocking mechanisms of the electric eel, an expert on the "landing gear" of birds, and the world's foremost authority on beetle mechanics.

HOW TO COMPENSATE THE EXPERTS

Be careful in the use of money. Not surprisingly, you can get almost anyone you want if you are willing to pay his or her asking price. The danger in this is that a session that should be an exciting, stimulating personal challenge can become just another consulting assignment if the individual is coming exclusively for his or her normal consulting fee.

This is why it's important to use other, less tangible incentives in order to get an individual to come, because he or she then feels intrigued, excited, and challenged. However, if the individual is being brought in for a typical consulting assignment, his or her full fee should be paid gladly.

USING EXPERTS EFFECTIVELY

There are a variety of modes that one can use to obtain knowledge, information, creativity, and insights from specialists. One common approach is a one-on-one event. Someone who has a number of questions or merely wants to be tutored in an area finds an appropriate specialist—typically a consultant—and brings him or her in to provide advice, training, or tutoring.

At the beginning of an assignment, we sometimes like to bring in a leading authority on an area to tutor us about some of the specifics with which we will inevitably be dealing. This is particularly true when the area involves specialized knowledge known only to a limited few. This can be an effective "jump start" on a getting smarter process.

Experts are also valuable in the quest for acquisitions. Specific, concrete material on potential acquisition candidates is typically very hard to obtain. Also, many potentially attractive acquisitions—particularly of emerging technologies or infant companies—are too small and new to be found in any literature. A person with a broad, in-depth knowledge and experience base in the area of interest can provide valuable time-saving perspectives and inside information, some of it gained via extensive networking. These tiny potential "plums" are seldom found in data bases or publications.

Another valuable use of experts is in debriefing, that is, assessing the output of an informational or creative session. Those responsible for this complex task often profit from having one of the expert participants spend additional time after the session to help in assessing information that may be technically beyond the comfortable grasp of the individuals who ran the event. Experts can also help clearly present and effectively support the results for the sponsoring client group or, within a company, the top management.

Another valuable use of specialized knowledge is when an organization already has a number of ideas that generate some degree of interest. In this case, bringing in outside specialists as a sounding board and bouncing these ideas off one or more of them can give an individual or group at least a quick preliminary feel for their potential value.

One way of accessing expert opinion without using a session event is via a carefully constructed expert survey. Here, carefully selected experts who agree to participate (about twenty) usually receive a fee. A survey is designed that will elicit the information sought, and this is mailed to the experts. Because each is a recognized leader in his or her field, the results are usually representative. And because the time spent in completing a survey is substantially less than what would be entailed in travel and a day of face-to-face conversation, the expert survey can definitely be cost-effective.

Finally, it should come as no surprise that we believe one of the most effective ways to use individuals with specialized, expert knowledge is within a session format. Some of the benefits are that this type of event intrinsically gets more out of the individual participants. The "electricity" generated when a group of bright people are brought together enhances their creative productivity and insights. There is an inevitable air of competitiveness that forces each participant to reach further into the resources of his or her subconscious mind.

Synergy results because of the huge pool of hard-earned knowledge that the group collectively brings. *Groups* don't have ideas or insights; every such product comes from the mind of a single individual. However, for some of the reasons just described, the session ambience greatly enhances this possibility.

How to Interact with Your Experts

Kurt Eastman, president of INNOTECH's Services Division, has a personal philosophy on dealing with experts: "Pamper them." Generally, invited experts will comprise a high-powered, well-reputed, affluent group. So when budgets allow, participants should be housed in more than adequate lodgings, be picked up personally, and so on.

Eastman also counsels, "Get to know them on a personal basis over a social event—dinner or lunch." This kind of VIP treatment pays off when they call up days, weeks, or even months after an event and contribute an additional piece of information or insight, or when they are needed for follow-up advice. Excellent relationships with these valuable resource people often pay dividends in the future.

Using Internal Experts

Trying to use internal experts for a one-on-one event or a lengthier session presents a number of unique challenges. First, because they are operating within their own organization, they usually feel comfortable and, therefore, tend not to bring the same dedication and electricity as outsiders to an assignment.

Also, often the task they are being asked to address falls into the category of "the same old problem." Political factors are often at play in and around the issue being focused on. Therefore, internal experts may be burdened with tons of "baggage" as they approach a familiar problem. All this presents difficulties, but they are not insurmountable if the appropriate creative steps are taken. An important technique is to disguise the problem creatively so that it does not *appear* to be the same old one.

Creative techniques, of which there are many, can go a long way toward forcing people to think of the assignment in new, different, fresh ways. But without an effective disguise or the intelligent use of appropriate creative techniques, the return on investment on a group of internal experts slamming into the same problem again can be low and very disappointing.

One simple way to influence insider dynamics greatly in a positive way is to add a few outside, independent, unbiased specialists with impressive credentials. This will electrify and change the dynamics of an otherwise difficult-to-run session. Unfortunately, these negative factors usually influence the productivity of sessions staffed exclusively with inside experts.

Almost always, however, there are ideas dwelling in the minds of the inside participants which either have not yet surfaced or, when they last did, were beaten into oblivion by negativity. Clearly, the only way they will surface is if the partici-

pants feel confident and comfortable that they are in supportive, friendly territory. This is where an experienced session
leader and the careful design and selection of the appropriate
techniques can play a key role.

A session of internal experts runs best when it is comprised
of peers. The attempt to combine high-level with low-level
participants produces pressures and tensions that can be insurmountable. An engineer will either be totally intimidated by the
presence of the vice-president of engineering or will run amok
with the sole objective of trying to impress him.

The responsibility for trying to make such an event work
definitely falls on the high-level individuals. They must set the
example by being nonjudgmental, uninhibited, and eager to
volunteer their ideas. If a senior-level executive can clearly
see how his or her attitudes and mode of participation will have
a positive or negative effect on a session, then there's at least a
chance of being able to conduct him or herself in a way that
enhances and does not derail a session of other insiders.

Finally, when an expert session is run using outsiders, there
is no obligation, need, or even value to getting back to them
with the results. It would be inappropriate, and it is not even
expected. However, this is exactly what needs to be done when
the event is run with internal experts. It is vital that we not
create a demotivating culture where it is understood that one
attends an event and that's the end of it. Mechanisms must be
set up to get results back to the internal participants. They are
part of the same team and, therefore, feel entitled to know
what benefits their contributions made in a session and what
the next move will be.

SEEING EXPERTS IN ACTION

A secondary benefit of bringing a group of experts together in
a session is that it allows you to see them in action within a
demanding, challenging, creative, and dynamic setting. In some

cases, invited experts are also potential job candidates. Thus, client executives sometimes purposely encourage the design of sessions that will allow them to assess a candidate's performance before hiring him or her as either an employee or a close-to-full-time consultant.

This was the case in a program conducted for Westinghouse Financial Services (WFSI), the financial arm of Westinghouse Corporation. WFSI was seriously considering moving into a related financial area and recognized its best strategy would be to hire a handful of carefully selected, highly qualified leaders in the various sectors required to put the organization together. A blue-chip team was staffed for the session event, which produced valuable information and insights to help shape the fledgling venture. However, another benefit was that WFSI's managers could designate which individuals to invite and then scrutinize their performance. This led to the hiring of some to form the initial core of the venture.

DESIGNING THE SESSION

By *session* we mean to cover the spectrum from a full-fledged expert session to a one-on-one meeting. Some components and principles apply to both and are critical to the successful outcome of any event that involves bringing together one or more specialists for the purpose of obtaining their potentially valuable contributions.

The first step is to establish the objective clearly. Every session we run has on the first page of the specially designed briefing document—and repeated two or three times within its fifteen to twenty-plus pages—a precise statement of the objective of the event. Knowing the objective will help you decide whether you really want originality (creativity), information, opinions, perspectives, or insights.

A factor that must be considered in light of the objective is whether a single session can adequately cover the required ground. Sometimes a focus is so broad that all the bases cannot be covered by bringing together seven or eight experts. In this case, perhaps the task will require two smaller sessions, each staffed with four or five individuals. Because the staffing must be specific to the objective, it is sometimes impossible, or at least dangerous, to try to cover too much in a single event.

PREPARING THE PARTICIPANTS

After the decisions about objectives and the number of sessions have been made, serious thought should be given to preparing the participants before the actual happening. As stated earlier, we favor the use of a carefully designed, thought-provoking briefing document. Without adequate, appropriate preparation, the event will be significantly less successful, regardless of the stature of the individual experts. Occasionally, we have had a participant arrive at a session without having received the briefing document, due to exceptional circumstances. He or she enters into the game disadvantaged and seldom catches up. Although these individuals may make some valuable contributions, they are hindered by not having had the right mental preparation.

Our experience also shows that because of the briefing document most participants will put in two to four hours prior to the session. These hours are powerful programmers of the subconscious mind, and the participants begin the session with valuable concrete information.

If the event is not a session but another type of interface, such as a one-on-one meeting, it's important that the attendee be informed of this in advance. There can be a significant emotional mismatch if an individual arrives expecting to be in a session and finds that the event is a full day of consulting, or vice versa.

If, for whatever reason, a briefing document is not created, a detailed agenda should at least be provided. Using the phone effectively to brief participants before a meeting also can be effective. If a participant has a question or insight prior to the meeting, he or she should be encouraged to call. This can then lead the session's sponsor to phone other participants with the clarification of a misunderstanding or with an elaboration of points.

EACH SESSION IS UNIQUE

There is usually little value in bringing a participant back for another similar session. Every session is a unique event comprised of a one-time, carefully selected group of participants. When the event is completed, the participants have contributed at least 80 percent of what they could possibly have brought to such a session. There may be valid reasons for using them later as interpreters, as experts to enhance credibility, or as members of the task force that will move a particular idea or opportunity toward commercialization.

However, bringing an individual back to participate in a similar event would essentially be a waste of time and money. Each session, well run and debriefed, will yield a subfocus much tighter than the original one. In turn, this subfocus will lead to an even more specific briefing document and the staffing of more "vertical" individuals precisely targeted to the subsequent objectives.

CHOOSING THE VENUE FOR THE EVENT

The right ambience and mechanical support can be critical to the success of an event. Assuming that these are adequately taken care of, the fundamental question becomes "where?" Many times information will have to be accessed from resources at a particular facility.

For example, if a consultant's office is filled with his or her personal library and reference materials, it may make sense to have the meeting there. Also, if the budget for a consultant's expenses is limited, it may be important to save on his or her travel. If, however, the entire output of a session is being debriefed and a room is filled with reference works, wall sheets, and samples, it probably would make far more sense to bring the individual to the debriefing site. Then there is always neutral ground. Most airports offer facilities adequate for small meetings. Also, the clubs and other meeting areas available in cities, or even dayrooms in hotels, provide fairly inexpensive options.

It is often of value to record meetings for more leisurely analysis. Recording a group session is imperative because things go by so quickly that more time is needed to conduct the "debriefing." Because it can be a bit difficult to listen to several hours of audio with a number of excited participants contributing and sometimes subgrouping, video is better. A video recording of the same event is easier to sit through and understand because body language and lips provide interest and clues to what is being said.

PULLING TOGETHER THE FACTORS

Optimizing experts starts by clearly setting forth objectives and, from there, deciding whether the involvement should be internal, external, or both. Again, preparation is 98 percent of the battle, because first-class preparation will practically guarantee that an event is productive.

On the other hand, casual—meaning little or no—preparation will guarantee the event will be of limited value, even if all the world's greatest experts were brought together.

Experts are people. Perhaps the drive that got them to their expert status has more ego needs within it. So these individuals, with their potentially valuable knowledge, must be treated with respect and attentiveness. Such care usually will prove to have been a good investment.

ANOTHER VIEW FROM THE REAL WORLD

Robert D. Duncan

Robert D. Duncan is group vice-president of PPG, with responsibility for its largest entity, the glass group. He first became involved with INNO-TECH's processes as head of the company's chemicals group.

Bob has a great interest in the effective use of outside resources and creative thinking. He was the de facto prime mover of a Planned Growth *program that resulted in PPG's move, via acquisition, into the area of specialty surfactants.*

You Have to Work at It

What I found in working through our growth process was that creativity is hard work. The results don't come easy. The idea that one can put groups together and have them come up with all those wonderful creative ideas is naïve. You get what you "pay" for! Further, it doesn't help when I have a problem within PPG to try and avoid the work by going out and hiring a consultant. Because when you get the consultant's output, in order for it to be meaningful, you still have the same amount of work to do to assimilate it. The same thought processes have to be put into it.

When we have problems, usually one of the big things missing in our business is a lack of rigor or attention to details. And creativity is no exception to that. It's a fallacy when people feel they can lay the responsibility for creativity in the laps of R&D and say, "You're the ones who are supposed to be creative; it isn't my job." And our R&D people are anxious not to fall into that either. How do they fall into it? I believe that creativity and invention stem from the same basic principles that make other things work in your company—attention to details and the proper organization of your thought patterns. Thomas Edison, among others, believed that creativity was 98 percent perspiration and only 2 percent inspiration. So when we look at the process we used, our success started with our commitment. The leader really has to think through what it is he's trying to accomplish before hiring the consultant. You've got to think that through in enough detail to be really committed to following through and spending sufficient amounts of your own time in the process. Clearly, you've gotten your people involved in the process to make it work. So it all starts there.

It Starts with the Leader

How do you get originality from employees and consultants? I believe it starts with the leader analyzing and understanding the problem and clearly establishing what he or she expects to get out of the process. All this takes time and effort, but that's how you get commitment. Once you have the commitment, you go out and look for an outside organization and say, "Okay, come on in here; I'm not looking for an easy answer; I've got something I need to understand and I'm committed to making this work and I need your help." Then, with that, you can make something go. If the leader is personally going to analyze the problem and really understand it, then his people will work to understand it. And, they're going to have a commitment because you have a commitment. It all works together and creates an atmosphere that "breathes" ownership, creativity, and all the other good things. So I've come to appreciate that there's very little that we do as business executives that doesn't fall under the fundamentals of blocking, tackling, and perspiration. You can't walk away from these things. The leader can't just turn them off and say, "Here's a mushy problem; go fix it. Do the magic." Yet we keep trying to.

I don't think there are any new answers. The answers are all the same. We keep struggling and looking for different answers and different ways to get at our problems. But they all come back to the same thing—fundamentals. Management is people, and people are the company. And if they understand the leader's vision and his or her commitment to that vision, then good things will happen. In Chemicals, we had a mission statement that was our way of trying to bring the organization to say, "Hey! We *do* have a vision."

The Need to Get Serious

Growth was and is an obvious problem. So you say, "Okay now we're going to address this problem by bringing in someone to help us lay the groundwork for growth. This is something important that's consistent with our vision, and I'm committed to it." This sets the tone for all the hard work that needs to be done. Through the process, through the use of an outside organization, I think I was able to say, "We really mean business!" I believe that the outcome in terms of specific projects was not as important as the use of the growth process to establish a commitment. If you've already really laid the groundwork for it, hiring a consultant or outside organization says, "These people are serious about this." The leader has to have this commitment, and because he or she has it, *everybody* pays attention. If he just hands the problem over and says, "Hey, folks, go solve this," it's not the same thing at all. They just go back to doing what they like to do or what they are forced to do due to everyday pressures. But because the leader is beating the drum and is seriously committed, they get committed. So I think that not only do we spend a lot of time looking for the "magic answer," but all to often we also delegate the search.

Management has to establish the vision and the direction for any organization. People have to understand where the organization has got to be in the future and, supported by the leader's commitment and encouragement, believe that it can get there. Then management has to be personally involved with the creative process. You just can't delegate it. We have consistently seen failure when the top people just walk away from it. It just doesn't happen. So, the issue fundamentally comes back down to leadership. If the top person is not pointing the direction and saying "Follow me!" nobody is going anywhere. Everybody wants to be a hero. So if you know where the leader wants to go, and you help get him there, you know you're going to be a hero. On the other hand, if you don't know where he wants to go, how can you be a hero?

You Need Lots of Ideas

It's important to let people know that you're not looking for the magic answer, because there aren't any. But there are a lot of ideas, all looking for the right home. You've got to get people to understand that in the process it's okay to make a mistake. We're not looking for win or lose. What we're looking for are the creative connections. And the connections come first from generating a lot of ideas—as many as you can—and then playing these through the process and against the criteria to find the right ones. We may generate a thousand ideas, and there may be no home for them right now. But if we get a thousand ideas, the likelihood of finding homes for three or four is much greater than if you start with only one or two ideas.

One of the things I got out of our program was what I call "The Rule of Ten." We promulgated it to our managers working on new projects in commercial development and research. Its purpose was to set a tone by acknowledging that we were going to make mistakes. We said we'd like to have ten business opportunities for the Chemicals Group to work on that had the potential of achieving x. The premise was that we were trying to encourage people to say, "Hey! X doesn't have to be very big." We knew that ten were not going to win, but maybe half of them might.

So you're greatly increasing your odds by spreading out with multiple ideas and programs. This was really, in effect, back to the quantitative aspect of creativity and the establishment of an environment that said we don't have to be perfect. There are going to be mistakes, and there are no easy answers. But we're going to play this thing out for the long haul.

I knew it would be hard work. But I knew we weren't going to go out and make one big acquisition that would solve all of the Chemicals Group's problems. We were going to do our homework and begin to develop ideas and create technologies that could become business opportunities. We were even willing to admit some failures, because we knew that all business opportunities don't come to fruition. So you want to talk realistically in terms of precisely what your business *could* be.

The Value of a Vision

A long-haul orientation is absolutely critical to the process. When the pressure builds, you say, "I've got to have growth now, so I'll go for a quick hit." This stifles the very creativity you need. The openness and the willingness to take risks disappear. So you've got to have the long-term perspective and say, "We've got a vision; we're committed. We're in it for the long haul, so let's don't panic. Don't look for the magic idea now, let's use The Rule of Ten." Then delegate the authority to others to manage those businesses. Let them know they're part of something that's going to help us all get where we need to be—and that the task will be a challenge. If it's "a piece of cake," you don't get the same emotional commitment. They've got to know this is the key game and we've got to win it. The Rule of Ten also keeps you from narrowing down too early. If you're down to one idea or opportunity too early and you get a failure, you've got nothing. So keep a number of options open—not the whole world, but a reasonable number.

The Leader *Must* Be Involved

If you create the right atmosphere, creativity can take you where you want to go. You can say, "There are some things we could spin off of what we're already doing." That's the creative process. Once you get in it and you get involved, you get people thinking about these things. Then you can spin off all sorts of opportunities. It's all interconnected because, there's more than short-range thinking—there's visibility and knowledge of how to be a hero. It all fits together. Innovation for business growth is a macro management system problem, and there's no one answer.

Finally, in order to get originality from both consultants and employees, the leader has got to be involved intimately in the process and help set the atmosphere. I'm sure that an awful lot of executives are not going to like hearing this. I don't like to hear it either. But if you don't have the time for the necessary level of involvement with an outside organization, then you might as well not hire them. Because then, far from optimizing their value, you're just wasting time on both sides. When you're talking about creativity and innovation, you're talking about dealing with a process and creating an atmosphere where you can generate ideas and opportunities for companies. And because it's a process, it demands personal involvement. Even when creativity is not involved—when you hire an expert to provide information—you still have to work hard to make sure that everybody understands exactly what information you want. In our case, INNOTECH had a unique process. We couldn't have done without it, but the process needed our intimate involvement. So to optimize the use of outside or even inside experts, you've got to have worked on your problem enough to be able to say; "Look here's my problem. I *understand* it, but I don't know how to solve it. I need your help."

9

COMMERCIALIZING NOVEL IDEAS
How to Go for it
(and When Not To)

You probably know Murphy's law: If anything can possibly go wrong, it will—and at the worst possible time. Many people who have been involved in the commercialization of a novel idea strongly believe that Murphy was an optimist! Given the myriad unknowns and things that can go wrong in the commercialization process, many executives and venture capitalists apply a rule of thumb to all plans and proposals submitted to them. It simply states that one must cut the sales projections by half and double the time estimates. Others who are possibly more pessimistic, or just more realistic, go further and cut the sales by two-thirds and triple the time required.

One indisputable fact about commercializing something novel is that one will *never* have all the answers at the outset. Given the realities, it takes an exceptional human being with an intense emotional commitment—a true champion—to guide a novel idea through the mine fields of commercialization. We used to refer to this person as the "kamikaze pilot," and few people sought that role. As has always been the case, anyone who views the task as just another job will rarely last or be successful.

BUSINESS PLANS AS FAIRY TALES

Although no one yet has been able to predict the future accurately, this has not deterred the writers of business plans. One business executive with extensive experience in new ventures used the adjective *absurd* in describing business plans. Some of the problem lies in optimistic, but inaccurate, figures. However, the most important shortcoming of business plans is that they cannot address the totally unexpected, unknown aspects of the future. Any presenter who claims to know where his or her novel idea or startup will be at any particular point in the future is at least suspect.

There have been many attempts to try to compensate for the inability to see clearly into the future. One is the game of "What if?" formalized with the label of sensitivity analysis. Again, the problem is that we're seldom smart enough to ask the right "what ifs." The placebo effect of a lot of "hard" numbers in a plan is interesting because the numbers themselves are usually best guesses. But their dubious merit is that they tend to placate someone.

ASSESSING THE FIT WITH A CORE BUSINESS

Ideas can be commercialized within a core business or set up totally independently as stand-alones. Typically, the truly novel idea suffers from being housed within a large, traditional core business. On the other hand, a closely related opportunity can logically fit and profit from being commercialized by individuals in a business with relevant skills and knowledge.

However, there are reasons that make greater independence from an ongoing business potentially valuable. Some of these might include that the new thing requires a commitment and pace not to be found in the larger entity. Or the political climate towards the fledgling effort is actually or potentially hostile. And there are others.

Typically, the further away an opportunity is from the knowledge and skills of its parent, the more independent it should be. The development of the Sunhook line of plant-hanging hardware profited markedly from the parent company's great strengths in the design and manufacturing of small die castings; the development of the Qualiplus line of high-speed visual inspection systems was set apart from its corporate parent, a large can manufacturer.

The road to success is not always so smooth, however. One problem is a preoccupation with an idea's fit with a core business. This point is critical when the new idea will be commercialized within a core business, but otherwise it may not be so important. In fact, if the promising new opportunity cannot be well served by the core business's existing capabilities, the developers would be far better off setting it up as a separate, stand-alone entity. However, quite often the bias with a promising idea is to adopt it, hence the phrase, "A good idea has many fathers." But forcing it into the wrong core business can be so detrimental as to kill it.

Three factors, then, need to be recognized with an idea that really does not fit a core business.

1.   The idea may be rejected because it doesn't fit.
2.   The idea may be forced to fit into the wrong environment.
3.   Management will often be reluctant to allow the idea to be developed as a stand-alone entity.

In support of letting a startup stand alone, we sometimes ask, "What were your company's sales in its first year of existence?" The answer is always a much smaller number than the present size of the existing business. Thus the point is made that small startups grow into large companies.

On the other hand, a core business may be serving a market that is dying. All the creativity, hard work, and money in the world will not reverse the inevitable demise. The town of Springfield, Massachusetts, perhaps with tongue in cheek, at one time displayed a sign announcing that it was the Buggy Whip Capital of the World.

Yet we see companies in such situations spend all their money and energy propping up a failing business and attempting to avoid or ignore the inevitable. We've seen entire national economies dedicated to such efforts. For example, because of a concern for continued employment, Scandinavia in the 1970s spent millions in vain attempts to keep declining industries alive. Had these funds been spent more creatively to replace one steel-making concern with 100 small startups, the economic outcome could have been far more resultful.

MARKET FOCUS IS CRITICAL

In the bad old days under laissez-faire R&D management and promiscuous idea generation—conducted in an environment where focus was never mentioned—some companies felt they had too many ideas. Clearly, commercializing an idea tends to be a time-and dollar-consuming activity. So they couldn't all be commercialized, though many were worked on.

Fortunately, much of this has changed. A decade ago, companies started hearing that market focus was important, so they talked a lot about it. Today, more and more organizations are actually *doing* something about it.

Matt Calish, an INNOTECH vice-president, believes that perhaps one reason is the great and visible successes of the Japanese, who are doing an outstanding marketing job right under our noses. As we have become continuously aware, they invent little of what they market, yet their remarkable success has literally put us out of business in certain areas. So, perhaps painfully, they have showed us the merits of a market-focused orientation. If marketing can be that important, it's more than critical in the commercialization of a novel idea.

COUNT ON BEING WRONG

Most probably, original assessments and estimates of market factors will be wrong. It's easy to come up with a poor estimate on size of market for a product that has never been sold. Although some forecasters might be honest enough to acknowledge a plus or minus 20 percent variation, reality would probably be better served in many cases by plus or minus 200 percent!

Interestingly, we can even be wrong about the person we think will be the buyer or user of our product or service. Some markets will never yield a clearly defined buyer because there are many potential levels of buying influence. This is more true with industrial or technical products, but it applies even with consumer goods.

Identifying the real buyer is critical, however, in designing ways to take any product to market. Having identified the wrong buyer or user leads one to attempt to sell in an inappropriate way. So a rational starting attitude is to assume that there is a reasonable probability that one might have erred on any one of these factors—plus others not even considered.

KILL FOR MARKET FEEDBACK

Given that there will be an enormous amount to learn on both the product and market sides, you must do everything possible to develop and maintain intimate contact with customers and users in order to obtain invaluable feedback. You can only modify or fix what you know is wrong, and you will find out little of that in your office.

Any venture manager or other key individual involved in an effort to commercialize something novel who can be found in his or her office just doesn't understand the situation. This is especially true during the early launch phase, because this is the time when the highest potential for learning exists. You must be totally flexible in order to examine, modify, and change expectations based on original premises. You must simply *live in* the market.

Given that few products are commercialized without having been technically developed and judged capable of being manufactured, the demise of a new enterprise can almost always be attributed to a failure to understand the customer or the distribution. Even when the novel idea is in the earliest development phase, getting smarter about the market should be pursued in parallel. Companies have lost enormous amounts of money and time by waiting for the development to approach completion before going out into the targeted market.

Any early information coming out of the marketplace can be extremely useful; it can be fed back into the development process and used to refine the product for greater market acceptance. But going back to a core principle of creative thinking—separating creativity from judgment—one must be forewarned that *negative* feedback from the market can have an emotionally debilitating effect on those who are trying to convert an idea into a commercial product or service. Even realizing that negative feedback is extraordinarily valuable, it still may be hard to take, especially if the idea's creator or others having a large emotional commitment in an idea are on the firing line absorbing this negative feedback. At least being forewarned is being emotionally forearmed. An alternative approach is to assign the initial, usually tough, market contacts to a separate individual or group. Optimally, however, the developer or prime movers should hear these comments firsthand to benefit fully from them.

SELLING THE FUNDING SOURCE

The president of ABU, famed Swedish purveyors of sport fishing equipment, told us that the first thing a new lure design has to catch is the *fisherman!* Likewise, unless the champion is independently wealthy, it is inevitable that at some point a cogent, coherent plan will have to be developed that contains sufficient information to sell the funding source.

Because business plans are necessarily filled with essentially soft information and unrealistic promises, as we've noted, it is probably helpful to put together a strong operational plan, too. In pursuing a novel idea, checkpoints and milestones are more useful than prose, however eloquent. It is not inconceivable that a novel idea can turn into a black hole from which individuals and funds will never reemerge. Consequently, realistic goals for key accomplishments need to function as a safety net before the strong force of emotional gravity sucks everything in.

Even a large, sophisticated, and successful organization such as Polaroid was almost put under by the totally dedicated commitment of its founder, Edwin Land, to develop instant motion pictures, despite the advent of video-cassette recorders. Because Dr. Land "owned" the company, the pursuit of this opportunity continued beyond the normally allowable period. So realistic milestones, complete with dollar and time limits, seem to be a rational safeguard against situations that intrinsically demand a high degree of emotional commitment, which can, in turn, blind the perpetrators to large warning signals and stop signs.

MAKE YOUR MISTAKES AS FAST AS POSSIBLE

As we've learned, fast mistakes typically mean small expenditures of time and money and, therefore, can be viewed as positive feedback. One of the most famous pieces of advice that circulates within the 3M Company, and has been taken to heart by others, is the phrase "Make a little, sell a little." This may not be possible in certain industries, as with a pilot plant to prototype the production of a new chemical material, but the goal remains to move as quickly and as cheaply as possible.

Trying to "make a little" will yield valuable information about feasibility, price, time, and so forth. Once some of the product exists, trying to "sell a little" will provide similar valuable information about the customer, user, distribution, pricing, and so forth. So whenever possible, it makes good sense to follow 3M's advice.

Keep in mind that the first time you provide the service or deliver the product you will inevitably discover a number of major or minor problems. If you are really committed to the ultimate successful commercialization of the novel idea, one of the best investments you can make is to provide stand-on-your-head, legendary service in order to rectify the problem or difficulty to the purchaser's satisfaction. The enormous benefit of such an outstanding service orientation, in addition to building a reputation and leaving a potentially disgruntled customer impressed and happy, is that it is a terrific vehicle for obtaining the most valuable commodity in the successful commercialization of a product or service—*customer feedback.*

Even if your initial offering has so many "bugs" it fails miserably, the customer who has been treated in a way that leaves him or her a friend will be more than willing to try the new, now debugged product. On the other hand, if a company's managers walk away from their early messes, the chances of reentering the market, at least with the same customers, are slim.

LOOK LARGER THAN LIFE

A novel idea is almost always viewed with at least some suspicion because it is unfamiliar to the buyer or user. Given the human tendency to love the familiar, the known, or the proven, developers of a novel idea need all the help they can get to convince the user to buy and try it. The stability, reputation, and prestige of a large, established organization are a terrific plus, even if the idea is unrelated to its current business.

We were told by a top executive in Westinghouse Corporation that the reputation the company had gained over the years through its high-quality offerings of both consumer and industrial products created a halo effect around the efforts of its Financial Services Company to operate in the Japanese economy, providing new financial services. Clearly, brand X Financial Services Company would have an extremely difficult job establishing the same image of stability and quality that was instantly available to Westinghouse.

So the goal is to attempt to find a name or create an image that will look larger than life to the user or buyer, thus helping to overcome initial resistance. One way to accelerate this image building is to operate at the highest level of ethics with customers, users, and distributors. Positive stories travel almost as fast as negative ones, which we all know travel faster than light. The best proprietary assets an organization can have are the intangibles of its name, reputation, and image for quality service.

RENT, DON'T BUY

Many companies operating in their traditional core businesses have both manufactured and sold their products themselves. Therefore, they can be quite naïve about what it takes to bring a novel, unrelated idea to market. Their knee-jerk reaction is to start to design, staff, build, and train a marketing organization and sales force. However, it is almost impossible to find a product or service—even the most novel—that cannot fit into some form of existing distribution, at least for a period of time.

The Sunhook line of plant-hanging hardware serves as an example here. The company's traditional distribution and sales strengths were directed to industrial users of small precision die cast parts. However, the new product line would be sold directly to the consumer. Without too much difficulty or time, a specialist in the consumer marketing of plant care products was found and did an outstanding job of establishing exactly the right networks and mechanisms to bring the line to market successfully.

SAMPLING

Although it might be a painful thought, one proven approach to launching a superior novel idea is to give it away under the right circumstances and to the right people. This effort must be well targeted to qualified buyers and must not extend beyond a reasonable introductory period. This approach can be extremely effective if the novel idea will be met with price resistance. The organization must be very confident that the product is so good that after initial use the customer will regularly purchase more.

Such was the case in the launch of RapidPurge, a novel, cost-effective product for helping operators of plastic processing machinery change colors or clean their equipment quickly and efficiently. The product was necessarily expensive, yet it was truly superior. So the decision was made to give it away—to provide samples to targeted customers.

The strategy proved effective. It also forced the creation of some rational guidelines about who should be sampled and how much should be sampled. In addition, it established the need to get a commitment from the targeted customers to actually *use* the sample. Free samples of superior products that are never used don't sell much product.

FORGET ABOUT PROFITS

One of the most common ways that company executives shoot themselves in the foot when it comes to commercializing novel ideas is that they become too profit oriented too early. Forgetting or ignoring that a fledgling business will not grow overnight to the size of their existing business, they measure performance by profits in the new business just as they do in all their old businesses.

Therefore, as soon as there seems to be any glimmer of market acceptance and potential success, they turn on the screws in an attempt to squeeze out profits. The first victim of this thinking tends to be the marketing and sales budgets, and the development and engineering efforts follow. All of these are critical to the further growth and success of the fledgling entity; consequently, it may be rather short lived.

This brings us back to patience—the patience required for doing something new. Many times, management grudgingly allocates monies to support a new enterprise and can't wait for its first commercial sales in order to stop the flow of funds. But such premature weaning will almost inevitably bring its demise.

WATCH THE COMPETITION

Another threat to a fledgling enterprise is competition. A novel idea will attract much attention, and before long competitors will be on the scene. Every effort must be made to have up-to-the-minute information on the offerings and strategies of competitors.

We hear phrases such as "marketing warfare," because a competitor's improvement can be quickly adopted, taking away the potential advantage. The best defense against competition is to start developing and generating improvements immediately—which, as most companies know, is a never-ending activity. Developers of a novel idea who think they can rest on their laurels while the market continues to clap, cheer, and buy are encouraging a takeover by aggressive and creative competitors.

Sometimes, people express concerns about prematurely exposing a promising idea through expert-to-expert sessions. In our experience, this potential danger is grossly overrated. Remember that participants can be selected on the basis of their willingness to sign a standard confidentiality agreement. The probability of a top-level professional knowingly violating a contractual obligation and then miraculously raising the capital and support to commercialize an idea illegally is very low.

Simultaneous Invention

There is a far more real danger: simultaneous invention, or organizations coming up with the same idea at essentially the same time. Simultaneous invention is a wild card that makes the game of finding and establishing a novel idea even more difficult. Companies moving forward with great confidence, spending enormous amounts of money to commercialize a seemingly novel and protectable idea, can find to their last-minute horror that a competitor is launching an almost identical product.

The only real protection for a novel idea is speedy commercialization. Everything that went into the creation of the idea—the analysis of market trends, the supporting technology, the processes, and so on—was theoretically available to others. If a company is fortunate enough to base a new product on its own proprietary technologies, materials, or processes, then clearly it has a much better chance of achieving the truly protectable product. But evidence tells us that if such a product is profitable and has a large market, enormous amounts of money and creativity will be targeted to get around any protective barrier.

Simultaneous invention may not always be bad news. During the early 1970s when there was much more emphasis on the creation of novel ideas as growth vehicles, programs often produced one or more ideas worth exploring. These were subjected to in-depth analyses and studies of marketability. But one benefit of having a specific idea in mind is that it produces a tight focus for a search. Quite often, before too much time had passed, these efforts revealed that either a small company, startup, single inventor, or university team was already working on this same, or a closely related, idea.

This discovery of the idea's existence was greeted as bad news, and the feeling was, "Someone beat us to it." Over the past several years, the reaction has more often led to efforts to acquire, license, or even form a partnership. In almost all cases the logic of this strategy is irrefutable. Some companies have all but abandoned internal development for growth avenues they judge to be faster and safer.

IS IT PROTECTABLE?

Concern for the theft of a proprietary idea at one end of the spectrum, and legitimate concerns about strong competition, lead most companies to a strong commitment to the protectable. Although the novel idea lends itself most naturally to protectability, there are other ways of achieving this highly desirable state without the cost and risks involved in internal development of a novel idea. Some of these are patents, art (proprietary secrets), exclusive license, and lead time.

Earlier in our industrial history, patents provided almost iron-clad protection of a novel idea. Unfortunately, this is no longer the case. Patents are often violated with impunity as companies realize that the settlement amount may well be equivalent to a licensing fee. By blatantly violating a patent, they are in essence forcing a license out of the patent holder. Consequently, organizations that formerly filed many hundreds of patents have greatly reduced their activity or even abandoned the practice. Some recognize that the information that will be published as a consequence of filing for a patent will disclose both the patent claim (allowing competitors to work around it) and the process or technology enabling it. Therefore, they feel that keeping the formula under wraps provides better protection of confidential information.

Interestingly, we find that a company's culture typically has a bias either for or against patents. Some companies recognize the inherent flaws in the system and view patents as baseball trading cards to pass among each other. This seems particularly true in the chemical industry, where a vast network exists in which every company seems to be a supplier, customer, licensee, and licensor of every other company.

Small companies, on the other hand, are more reluctant to invest the dollars and time required to pursue patents because they realize that a patent is only as strong as the resources they're willing to commit to protect it. This sometimes leads to a bullying of the little guy, because large organizations can hurl their batteries of lawyers against the essentially defenseless small organization.

If a company has a patented idea, obtaining an exclusive license for it—whether broadly or narrowly market focused—gives the licensee the ability to hide behind the coattails of the licensing parent. This can be an effective strategy for companies and provide them with a proprietary position in a novel idea without having to develop, own, or protect it themselves.

Finally, some strong, marketing-oriented companies are so confident of their ability to establish market dominance, given a head start, that they view having a certain amount of lead time on their potential competitors as akin to a proprietary position. There is no doubt that the marketing muscle of some companies is truly awesome—Gillette comes to mind. In one meeting the response to a question about key strengths produced the reply; "We know how to get a product on the shelf, and we know how to get if off."

PEOPLE MAKE IT HAPPEN

Years ago we were naïve enough to think that if a novel idea was given to a willing and accepting corporate staff, success was only a matter of time. Much to our chagrin, this repeatedly proved to be wrong. Everyone in the company already had a full-time job; therefore, attempting to commercialize the novel idea was just another burdensome responsibility. Often, it was far more expedient to prove quickly that the idea was not viable and should be killed off so that everyone could go back to his or her core responsibilities. In other cases, sincere individuals genuinely tried their best but could not steal suficient time for long enough to give birth to a successful opportunity.

The two critical roles in the successful commercialization of an idea are those of the champion and the sponsor, whose roles we have discussed in previous chapters. The champion, of course, is the prime mover responsible for getting a project to its conclusion. The sponsor helps the champion move safely through the dangers of corporate politics and fulfills other critical roles such as that of sounding board, confessor, and friend. Executives who are overseeing the commercialization of a new idea tend to "keep pulling up the plant to see if it's growing." The sponsor's should have so much credibility with the management group that he or she can report to them regularly on how well the plant is doing, and thus protect the fledgling's growth.

Things that motivate businesspeople include money, challenge, recognition, and praise. Because no organization is comprised of a homogenous group of individuals motivated by the same forces, *all* motivators must be used effectively. Intrinsically, however, the challenge and excitement of successfully taking a novel idea into the marketplace has the greatest *potential* for generating enthusiasm and commitment from all the participants. This process is far from a given, however, and the wrong "style" coming from a sponsor or champion may produce the opposite effect and lead to failure of the enterprise.

Management must provide motivation and leadership for the champion. It is difficult to use conventional performance standards such as bonuses based on profits in a wholly new enterprise. What usually works most effectively is to reward individuals for their achievement of milestones, because profitability may be a long way off.

Once the business is in operation and growing, it still may make good sense for a period of time to reward the champion on the basis of top-line sales rather than bottom-line profits, which typically remain elusive during the startup investment phase. (This is especially true in large-company ventures where establishing market position—and share—is significantly more important, in the short run, than simply making profits.)

STAY LEAN ON PEOPLE

Typically, the small size of the team and the clarity of its task, mission, and vision create potential for employee enthusiasm and commitment. However, it takes the right management and leadership style to realize these. Enthusiasm and commitment are aided by remaining lean. Overstaffing early on can be detrimental. Sometimes affluent organizations immediately hire someone full time for a responsibility requiring only half time or less at this phase. Given that most of the people in a startup will be working at 150 percent of capacity, an individual work-ing at a half-time role for full-time compensation is a drag on morale. Hiring part-time help, however, is not only a more effective use of funds but also, under the right circumstances, often an excellent opportunity to preview a potential full-time employee. This "preview" concept should be kept in mind with any part-time or consulting personnel.

A mechanism for bringing experience and perspective to the commercialization of a novel idea is to set up an informal, genuinely supportive board or council to meet regularly with the prime movers on the firing line. Properly established and used, such a formal, consultative body can be valuable for a host of reasons—certainly it's a way of increasing the confidence in, and thus the implementation time of, new ideas and deci-sions. (A caveat is to make sure that the growth team is not iso-lated and does not become incestuous.)

There may be a temptation to stay in the comforts of the office supported by loyal fans, rather than brave the harsh winds of negativity and criticism in the marketplace. Painful as it might be, it is invaluable to live in the marketplace and obtain the precious feedback that can mean the difference between success and failure.

WHEN *NOT* TO GO FOR IT

Attempting to commercialize a novel idea takes a great deal of commitment, dedication, and emotional energy. Superimpose on this, the positive, can-do attitude needed to overcome the many obstacles, and the critical issue, in poor developmental situations, becomes *when* to finally throw in the towel and admit that this particular novel idea will never fly.

Massive dosages of creativity dollars and enthusiasm can go a long way in turning almost any problem into an opportunity. But there are times when even these are not enough. An idea may need to be dropped if, after extensive searching, it is clear that there is no market need or an insufficient market need, or

that the required pricing shrinks the market too much to justify continuing.

Such a realization may be derived from the fact that although
the product or service addresses a stated need, the frequency of
the need is so low that no one will pay the price, or the problem
is so minor that, again, no one will pay the price. (Paying the
price, you can see, is the critical decision point for any new
product or service.)

Unambiguous no-go signals emerge when technological hurdles prove insurmountable. If a product or service can't be made
or provided for a reasonable price, the market will not pay what
it considers too much for even an elegant technical solution.
Another factor that applies to technical hurdles might be that
during the development cycle, superior technology emerges
from a competitor that actually makes your product obsolete
before it is ever commercialized. Such "premature obsolescence" may not produce a dead stop, but it would certainly
throw the development back in time in order to pursue a new
avenue.

Once again this highlights the critical issue of the pace of
change. If the pursuit of the novel idea is proceeding in parallel
with competitors who are moving along the same avenue, the
race may simply be lost. And with the loss of the race to the
marketplace, economic factors may change enough to abort a
once promising project. Perhaps the key question is simply,
Are you truly competitive? Seldom can going forward with no
hope of developing some element of competitive advantage be
justified.

ANOTHER VIEW FROM THE REAL WORLD

John Mills

*John Mills is president of Firing Circuits, Inc., a manufacturer of sophisti-
cated, heavy-duty battery chargers for forklift trucks, robots, golf carts,
and other specialized battery-charging applications. He worked with*

INNOTECH during the early 1980s. The creative challenge was the development of a beyond-the-state-of-the-art intelligent electronic battery-charging system.

John's experience in commercializing novel ideas includes this "adventure," along with several years spent in the development and commercialization of many other new products and systems.

QUALIFY THE IDEA

Entrepreneurs and business leaders have ideas for doing something better. The ideas may result from the individual's special knowledge of a market or the evaluation of an existing product or service. Ultimately, its successful commercialization is heavily dependent on the estimation of its market impact. This may be a formal or informal process, but the idea's "father" must keep in mind that if investment is required, those investing will want to see proof that the product or service is desirable. Will the idea work? Will the results meet user expectations? What are the opportunities and barriers facing this idea? Answers to these questions will greatly affect the final design, marketing, and selling decisions.

What Resources Will It Require?

After determining as best as possible the expected market acceptance of the new product or service, the next key area of concern is, What resources will it take to fully develop the idea to its successful completion? Almost everyone underestimates. Questions one must ask include: What specific knowledge must we have to fully develop the idea? Do we have the personnel or resources available with the knowledge required? If not, where will they come from? How long do we estimate for the development process? Will disruption occur to the normal business flow during this development? How much will the development cost? How long will it take to recover our investment from sales of this new product or service?

It's very important that the originator of the idea be fully involved with the planning of its development and the initial marketing. There are a lot of other questions to ask, but these are some we dealt with when we began the commercialization of our own novel idea—the Life-Plus electronic battery charger. I believe that the inventor or prime mover must champion the program through to the point of commercialization. That includes being involved in setting up the marketing requirements. If at all possible, the initial idea generator definitely should be the champion of the commercialization effort, because he's the one who has the emotional commitment. This is a crucial factor.

My experience with commercializing ideas has taught me that the greatest pitfall is underestimating by a factor of between two to three times the resources and time necessary to get the idea to market. That's because it's impossible at the beginning to conceive of all the development problems that lie ahead. The only things you get on your list, or in your plan, are what you know. What you *don't* know isn't going to be there. And that's what doubles and triples the time.

People and Culture

The first step in the commercialization of a novel idea is to decide who will lead the effort. If it can't be the creator of the idea, it should be someone with a good knowledge of all the disciplines required. The more this person knows, the better off you're going to be. It will be terribly costly, both in financial terms and time, if he's not the right person, and you may not end up with a product that meets your initial goals. This applies equally whether the novel idea is for a product or service. Whoever manages the program must be able to locate the technical, financial, and marketing resources that will be needed.

A company's culture definitely has an effect on the business of commercializing an idea. For example, is creativity going to be allowed during the development? Can we look down other avenues that might be different from the one for which the idea was originally conceived? Given this license, the commercialization process itself can enhance the creativity in an organization. Or if it's stifled, it might have a very adverse effect. The organization can put the blinders on and say, "Just get the thing out and don't bother me with any other ideas."

I've learned that when you develop and commercialize an idea, you should try to take it almost completely out of the corporate life so that the people involved in it are not forced to lead dual roles. It really needs its own space. One should definitely try and remove the activity from the day-to-day concerns of running the existing business. I believe that one of the benefits of doing this is that you'll have the greatest level of creativity going into it; you'll see more opportunities to build on the idea. Possibly other ideas will come out, and you'll end up with more than just one product. So creativity during the development is an important component of the commercialization process.

It's a Full-time Job

You need someone working full time on any major development of an idea. It can't be a part-time effort by personnel who already work in the organization or someone from the outside who has no real interest in the program. I'm not saying that you can't have some of those people involved. There may be some specific areas that only need help for short periods of time, and that's certainly acceptable. But the management of the program and the prime mover or movers must be able to devote full time to it without having to break off their thinking on a day-to-day or hour-to-hour basis. This full-time dedication greatly enhances the chances of coming up with the very best results from the novel idea—and even other ideas for products or services, because the starting idea is still in need of creative shaping and refinement, which may trigger other ideas.

These are some of the pluses, but there are also minuses from *not* having a full-time, dedicated champion on the project. One is that it seemingly takes forever to get the idea brought to commercialization—it runs well past any schedules that were originally put together. I think this is due to the constant breaking off of thought. Because of interruptions you end up having to redo things over and over again, which is a very inefficient way to work. So the cost of the project goes up considerably, simply because of the excessive time that goes into it. Again, you lose a lot of the creativity that would have otherwise been applied to the idea, and you may not end up with the best results in the end. I think that most often the root cause of a less-than-full-time champion is financial, that is, somebody *thinks* they're going to save money by not putting a person on it full time. But it's really going to cost them a lot more money due to inefficiencies. And there's no doubt in my mind about this whatsoever.

Ask the Tough Questions

Another critical question in the commercialization of a novel idea is, Can it really ever be commercialized into a product or service? That's the toughest question of all. Will the idea be accepted by the market where you intend to sell it? It's crazy to develop it before finding out if they want it. So you'd better find out whether they want it first, *before* you start to develop it. Everyone who comes up with an idea thinks at the start it's terrific. Then he or she often learns later on—or, hopefully, early on—that the idea is not workable because of a host of reasons, among them strong traditions that will prevent its acceptance, competition that's much stronger than you are in financing, or marketing mismatches in the stage of development.

The market questions are so important you can forget about technical feasibility or hardware for the moment. The key point I'm trying to get at is, should this idea even get to the point of development? Because that is question number one, and you can't ignore it. Just because an idea seems good to an individual, it doesn't mean it will fly in the marketplace. Then, if the idea has strong market merit, is it technically feasible? Can it be developed?

I have friends in the medical field who have come up with some new ideas for diagnosing diseases. They have super processes and absolutely brilliant ideas. But until the ideas are accepted by doctors, they have no chance of ever getting off the ground. The question is not only, Will it be accepted by the marketplace? but What will it take to get it accepted? Educating the marketplace is often overlooked, and it's probably one of the greatest expenses a novel idea has to endure. Unfortunately, some ideas are intrinsically almost impossible to market test beforehand. So if you can't get a good evaluation of the market acceptance of the product or service early on, my advice is stay away from it.

Another red flag is, Are there any technological barriers to the development of the idea? Maybe the idea can't be developed with the technology available today. Just because the market thinks it's a terrific idea, don't assume it can be developed. And the financials are *very* important. What's the return going to be on this product or service? Can we develop it in time? Will the cost be so great that it will take a period of sales beyond what its expected market life might be? If the inventor doesn't care, *someone* will want to know what the return on investment will be. Another question to ask is, Are all the necessary resources—technology, people, finances—available to bring this to completion?

To Bail out or Not?

One real problem we ran into on the development of our electronic battery charger system—the kind that sends you home with a knot in your stomach—was overrunning expenses and time. You put a lot into the program and then find that some of your technological obstacles still are not resolved. Should you bail out? I think we didn't at times when we should have. So there definitely need to be milestones during the development process. Even if the idea promises to be a great marketing success, if it turns out that during the development it looks like it's going to be far too costly to bring it to completion, you have to take a good hard look at it and say, "Should we go on?" And too often, because so much has already been put into it, you go forward with it. It's the classic problem of good money after bad.

There really are two key issues around "bailing out." The first question is, When *do* you bail out? And the second is, When *don't* you bail out? That's where those milestones are definitely required in your overall development plan. They enable you to ask, "Have I accomplished everything we said we should at this point?" You must do this all along the way. There should be at least a handful of these milestones in your plan. I'm not really too worried about bailing out when I shouldn't. What worries me more is that I won't bail out when I should. When we did bail out on other programs, it was always much later than we should have. But I've rarely heard of anybody who did it at the right time. It's *always* too late when somebody finally beats you on the head and says, "Look! Bail out!"

How Far ahead Should You Get?

On the product we developed with INNOTECH, we just did not recognize how difficult the technology for an intelligent battery charger was going to be. The development turned out to be four times more expensive than we'd anticipated and one and one half times lengthier. It was too much on the leading edge of the state of the art. We had trouble getting components because the concept was so far ahead of its time. And we had enormous difficulties all through manufacturing in being able to keep the quality of components coming in at the level that was required for a product that had to be highly reliable. Maybe in another few years the components that we put into the product will have higher reliability and be more readily available. At the end of last year we sold the product line off to another company. So far, that company is having much more trouble than we did. So what I learned was, don't go too far out on the leading edge.

Your culture plays a role here too. We always had a very creative climate within our group. Maybe too creative. So we had a tendency to go to the edge. But it's a real dilemma, because in today's field of electronics you find that change is so rapid that by the time you're finished developing a product, some of the component parts you're using are already becoming—or soon will be—somewhat obsolete. It's especially true on the computer side of the electronics involved.

I believe the "time window" of an electronic product today is that it its life cycle will probably be only two to three years. It definitely varies with the type of product, but that's the range if it's a computer product. If it's an industrial product, but still related to or makes use of computer electronics, it may last four to five years.

It's All about Marketing

Another problem that sent me home with knots in my stomach was marketing. Bottom line, the whole process of commercializing a novel idea is totally dependent on the marketing of the product or service. Some people say, "Well, it doesn't do all the things it's supposed to, but we'll market the hell out of it anyway." But you can't play that game for very long, because eventually they'll find out that the product doesn't live up to its marketing. Whatever it is, it must meet the expectations of the user. If it doesn't, you really have nothing to talk about. But assuming it does deliver, how it goes to market during the few years of its life is critical. You've got to work very fast with the best marketing vehicle that you can put together to get the greatest return from its sales potential. Anything less than that will reduce the return. If it's something that has to be sold through distributors, obviously you want an organization as good as you can put together. Whether it's distributors, mail order, or something else, a strong marketing plan and effort must be there to reach the product's expected volume. The world is definitely not going to beat a path to your door, I don't care how novel, terrific, or super you think the product or service is. If you're not out letting them know you're there, they won't know it—and you've got to let them know well, often, and loudly. But it's expensive! So you've got to be very efficient and effective in the use of your marketing dollars.

That was another area in which we made some poor judgments. Because of financial constraints we went through a single company for our distribution, and it proved not to have a strong marketing and sales force. So the product languished. Financial constraints have to be considered in the beginning. They may cause you to select less than the optimum marketing effort. Most people are used to investing in a technical development effort, but they often forget that marketing takes investment too. And with some products it could be much more costly than the technical development. So unless a company is willing to put that investment into it, the product may die simply because it wasn't marketed properly, not because it didn't work. Marketing is like fertilizer; if you don't fertilize a product or service, it won't grow well. So that was one of the biggest mistakes we made in the past, and certainly one we made with the intelligent battery charger.

There's No End to Commercialization

Finally, once you've been successful and grown an idea into a major factor in your business, it's not over. You'll be building on it for years to come. You can't just come out with a novel idea and think that's the end of it. If it's going to be something that's significant to your company, it will have to be followed through with continual development to provide the second generation, the third, and so on. So you have continuing marketing and development expenses. There's no end to "commercialization" if you want to maintain your position in the marketplace. Most people know these factors have to be considered, but even those who know them continue to forget them or come up with excuses and reasons why in this particular situation they should be violated. Then, later on, they relive the same terrible experience they had the time before. It's "Here we go again!" So as executives—and just as human beings—we tend to forget, we tend to make excuses, and we tend to violate all our own rules and principles. In fact, I'm not sure how much we truly forget, as opposed to how much we excuse ourselves from having to follow our own rules. And we excuse ourselves from our rules because we fall in love—we have a love affair with an idea. While we do, perhaps the industry is moving in another direction. So by the time we finish our development, it wandered away from the position that would have made it attractive, which again points to the need for speed in development. But while speed is very important, I have to come back again to the key factor—the initial market evaluation of the idea. It's got to be solid.

INDEX

ABOUT THE AUTHORS

R. Donald Gamache is one of the founders of INNOTECH Corporation, a company that provides consulting services to help companies grow into new areas and revitalize existing businesses. Mr. Gamache started working on practical applications of creativity to the needs of businesses in 1965. Since then, he and INNOTECH's professional staff have developed INNOTECH's Planned Growth process, a proven system of growth strategies that have successfully helped many corporations. Mr. Gamache's work has been the subject of numerous articles in the business press in the United States and abroad. He has also contributed writings to many business publications, including McGraw-Hill's *Handbook for Creative and Innovative Managers*, and Harper & Row's *New Directions in Creative and Innovative Management*. He is a graduate of St. Peter's College and served in the U.S. Army as a military intelligence officer.

Robert Lawrence Kuhn is an investment banker and corporate strategist at home in the complementary worlds of finance, business, academia, government, and media. Trained as a scientist, Dr. Kuhn is an expert in mergers and acquisitions, financial strategy and structure, as well as business creativity and innovation. He is editor-in-chief of the definitive *Library of Investment Banking* and *The Handbook for Creative and Innovative Managers*. He has written over twenty books on a broad range of subjects, including the new Ballinger book, *Investment Banking: The Art and Science of High-Stakes Dealmaking*. He holds a BA in human biology from Johns Hopkins University, an MS in Management from the Sloan School of Management, and a Ph.D. in Neurophysiology from the Anatomy and Brain Research Institute at the University of California, Los Angeles. Dr. Kuhn is currently a Senior Research Fellow in Creative and Innovative Management at the IC^2 Institute, University of Texas, Austin and also Adjunct Professor of Corporate Strategy in the Department of Management and Organizational Behavior, Stern School of Business, New York University.